15.

O

.E8

B 73:24

Sources
of
Illustration

# Sources
# of
# Illustration

1500 – 1900

*Hilary and Mary Evans*

*Adams & Dart*

*for Eric Benton*

© 1971 Hilary and Mary Evans

First published in 1971 by Adams & Dart 40 Gay Street Bath Somerset

SBN 239 00095 1

Printed in Great Britain by Redwood Press Trowbridge

# Contents

*All the illustrations in this book come from The Mary Evans Picture Library. The drawings of techniques are by Sheila Rand. The authors would like to acknowledge the help and advice they have received on the technical side from Eric Benton and Maurice Suckling; and, for assistance in compiling the list of sources, from Andra Nelki and Lynette Trotter.*

Portrait of John Thane (1748–1818), printseller and engraver. Engraved by Ogborne from the painting by Bigg. Not all collectors of illustrations are so elegant.

'To elucidate by means of pictures': this is only one of the definitions of the word 'illustrate', but it is the one that concerns us here. Illustrations as pictorial information, visual images with a practical function to perform, are what this book is about.

This function has been recognised from the earliest days: schoolbook and textbook illustrations are among the first printed pictures. But the history of illustration has seen a continual increase in quantity and broadening of scope, until in our own day we find ourselves placing considerable reliance on visual communication, whether to explain the complexities of a manufacturing process, identify a wanted criminal, indicate the lie of a landscape, or simply tell us more about the universe in which we live.

Another thing we notice in the historical development of illustration is a growing self-consciousness. For reasons which can no doubt be related to social psychology, we humans have grown more and more concerned to define and record, so that today we document the life of the worker in the coalmine as well as that of the queen in her palace, the misery of defeat as well as the glory of victory, the quiet pleasure of a suburban tea-party as well as the splendour of a state banquet.

Retracing our way through history, we find that such documentary material grows continually sparser. Every picture-researcher learns, early in his or her career, that there is little chance of finding direct documentation of everyday life in the age of Queen Elizabeth I, or even in that of Samuel Johnson. Such material has to be obtained obliquely, marginally—a city-scape glimpsed over the Madonna's shoulder in an otherwise unimaginative picture of the virgin and child, a domestic interior serving as background to an aristocrat's portrait. Most of our records of the trivia of the daily life of the past have been recorded in this accidental manner.

When we do actually come across an artist who concerns himself with the everyday lives of ordinary people—a Callot recording the miseries of the Thirty Years' War or a Honthorst depicting a visit to the dentist in the 1640s—we feel a bond of sympathy with the artist all the stronger because such concern is so rare. Rare—but not non-existent: this is something else the picture-researcher has to learn, and it is this that raises his job above that of a filing clerk. For of no subject can he say positively,'Such a picture does not exist'.The most he can say is, 'It is unlikely to exist, and as far as I know it does not exist'. But there is always the chance . . .

Recording contemporary history. The war artist of *La Guerre illustré* on a battlefield of the Franco-Prussian War, 1870; and Mr F. Villiers, special artist of the *Graphic*, lecturing in 1887 on his experiences during the Russo-Turkish War.

### The perennial theme: ourselves

Certain subjects have been copiously illustrated throughout history, people especially. Man has always taken an interest in his fellows, and one can find portraits from every age. Here, what we detect is a change of emphasis from one period to another. Kings and their ministers are always with us, of course, and so are generals and admirals as long as they are sufficiently victorious. When religious controversy is in fashion, we are inundated with portraits of religious partisans: among English portraits there are countless Puritan divines from the 1640s and innumerable staunch Protestants from the 1840s, when the Oxford Movement threatened a return to Rome.

The eighteenth century in Europe was the age of the individual man, and so we encounter a welcome change from kings and barons in eccentric misers and gallant highwaymen. The nineteenth century gave rise to heroes in less familiar fields—sporting heroes, industrial heroes, scientific heroes, even heroes of the temperance movement. And always, we find the artist himself as hero, understandably determined to preserve his own likeness along with that of his subjects.

Next to himself, man's interest is directed on the world in which he lives. The duke is proud of his palace, the burgher of his native city; so they are faithfully recorded for us. Towards the end of the eighteenth century, about the same time that he began to see each person as an individual, man discovered new qualities in his physical environment: so now we begin to get pictures of natural scenery as a subject in its own right. Changes in topographical illustration chiefly consist, apart from this, of changes in approach: Merian's picture of Paris in 1640 (**12a**) is documentation pure and simple; Throsby's drawing of Danet's Hall in 1789 (**34a**) is related to the new identification of man with nature; Shepherd's views of Metropolitan Improvements of 1829 (**45b**) are a monument of civic pride.

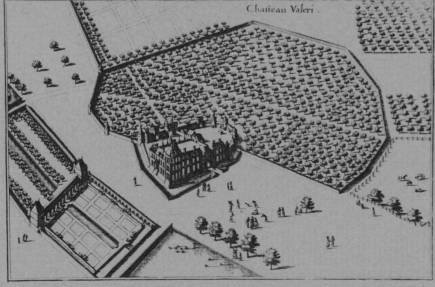

Nature with and without the human touch. A seventeenth-century bird's-eye view of the Château Valery (left), which shows the landscape neatly rearranged to suit a cultivated taste; and a view (above) of the Birks of Aberfeldy, by Hill, early nineteenth century, showing nature visited but untouched by man.

Wood engraving (originally coloured) after the tapestry at Bayeux

Copper engraving after a medieval manuscript

Steel engraving by Payne from the painting
by Philip James de Loutherbourg (1734–1812)

Wood engraving, with printed colour, by James Doyle
from his *Chronicle of England* (1864)

**Four views of the
Battle of Hastings, 1066**

There were no war artists in 1066: the present-day author who wishes to include an illustration of the Battle of Hastings must choose between such second-best versions as these. The Bayeux tapestry and the anonymous manuscript are of course closest in time to the event, and have a certain appearance of authenticity chiefly due to their antiquity. Loutherbourg, who specialised in battle-scenes commemorating the history of his adopted country, gives us a battle which is hardly to be distinguished from any of the other combats he painted. James Doyle's childlike version is in many ways the most convincing.

**Gluts and gaps**

Our knowledge of the past, based on the visual documents it has left us, is inevitably partial. Gluts in some fields are offset by tantalising gaps in others. We have more portraits of minor Flemish painters than we need, but we do not have a single authentic portrait of Christopher Marlowe. We have almost an excess of pictures showing the cruelties perpetrated by Queen Mary's Catholic bishops on the wretched Protestants; we would welcome a few more showing the equally cruel retaliatory actions taken by the Protestants. We shall never be absolutely sure what the interior of the Parthenon looked like; or under what circumstances Newton hit upon the existence of the force of gravity; or what the Battle of Hastings was really like. Even when contemporary illustration exists, it is often clearly untrustworthy; we have to ask ourselves whether it may not be safer to steer clear of contemporary pictures altogether, and make a graphic reconstruction of the event in the light of knowledge culled subsequently from other historical sources.

Until about 100 years ago this was in fact normal practice. To the best of our knowledge, the first comprehensive history book to rely exclusively on authentic historical illustrative material was Green's *Short History of the English People*, which was reprinted in an illustrated edition in 1892. Before that, the illustrations for history books were usually specially drawn—when, that is, they were not 'borrowed' from an earlier book.

It is certainly true that, thanks to a greater availability of data and an increase in technical skill, the reconstruction of a later age may well be more accurate than a record made at the time of the event. When we look at this seventeenth-century picture of the execution of Charles I we can see that the artist has got his perspective wrong, that the proportions of his Banqueting House are faulty, that the number of people in his crowd is wildly unrealistic, that his portraiture is sketchy to the point of meaninglessness. Yet none of this alters the fact that the contemporary record has a unique value which no reconstruction can give.

So long as we avoid the danger of thinking that there must exist a contemporary picture of every subject we would like, or that a contemporary illustration is of necessity reliable, we will find that an astonishingly rich variety of material *has* survived. One of the guiding principles in selecting for this book has been to indicate the scope that exists. Moreover, the quantity is continually increasing; not that it is being added to, of course, but more is being discovered and made accessible. In libraries, remote monasteries, private attics and the like, there undoubtedly remains a wealth of material unsuspected by most of us; and the sometimes maligned publishers of part-publications and coffee-table books are performing a useful service in sending their researchers to unearth material which has been forgotten or neglected. New techniques of communication mean that today we can make fuller and better use of illustration than ever before; technical innovation is leading to a new appreciation of the visual heritage of the past.

The execution of King Charles I, engraved after Sir Godfrey Kneller

An illustration is a picture with a purpose: it has to communicate information of some kind. To achieve that purpose, it must generally be made available in quantity. Apart from the rare instances where the original artist makes additional copies of his own work, this entails some sort of printing.

We can draw a broad distinction between two kinds of illustration:

*a.* Those that are conceived from the start as illustrations, and where the original is therefore in some reproducible form;

*b.* Those which start life as 'one-off' items, and so have to go through some kind of 'conversion' process before they can be reproduced. The tapestry on which this engraving from *Acta eruditorum* was based, for instance, may well be no longer in

Engraving from *Acta eruditorum* (1683), a German scientific journal, based on a tapestry of 1370 showing the court of the French King, Charles V.

existence; or if it is, it may be in private possession. Thanks to this engraving, however, a very interesting scene of the French medieval court has been made available for all. Clearly, though, it has lost a great deal in quality in the process.

Other things being equal, we are likely to find that an engraving of a picture drawn with reproduction in mind will possess a quality lacking in one which began life as a tapestry, a painting or a similar type of work. These two portraits of Columbus illustrate the point: Larmessin's version is far more vivid than the otherwise admirable steel engraving by Greatbach after the painting by Parmigianino.

As explained in the next chapter, there are many different ways of reproducing a picture. Each of them is a compromise between, on the one hand, the desire to preserve as perfectly as possible the quality of the original; and on the other, practical and economic limitations.

These limitations are responsible for a further complication—a picture may be created with one form of reproduction in mind, but later modified for another. For example, a metal engraving is more expensive to print than a wood engraving, because it has to be printed separately from the type-matter while the wood engraving can be printed at the same time. Until about 1825, this was not a significant factor, because wood engraving was not considered an acceptable alternative to

Two portraits of Columbus: one from Thevet's *Pourtraits et Vies des Hommes Illustres* (1574); the other an engraving by Greatbach (nineteenth century), after the painting by Parmigianino (1503–40).

metal; but the growth in popular demand for low-cost illustrated books completely changed the situation. In the first place, this new mass market was so anxious for illustrated material that it would accept lower standards of quality; and in the second place, publishers (largely inspired by the example of Thomas Bewick, *see* **38**) found that it was possible to improve the quality of wood engraving. The result was that wood engraving rapidly became the normal technique for popular illustration, metal engraving being reserved for superior work, where cost was not the primary factor. To begin with, illustrations were created specifically for the new technique, but inevitably it came about that publishers wanted to reproduce pictures which had existed as line engravings on metal, and this involved re-engraving the old metal engravings as wood engravings.

Queen Victoria and party taking a picnic lunch at Cairn Lochan, 1861. Steel engraving by James Stephenson from Victoria's *Leaves from our Journal in the Highlands*; wood engraving from the *Illustrated London News*. Both based on the same drawing by Carl Haag. At its crudest, the conversion process is well depicted by this pair of engravings. However, it is only fair to add that wood engravings were not always so blatantly inferior.

Another example of conversion is the re-drawing of some kind of metal engraving with a different technique in mind; this again was generally done for reasons of cost. The Hollar view of Westminster in 1647 was originally an etching, but its publisher, in 1809, to whom the original plates would almost certainly not be available, preferred—good etchers not being so easy to find as good engravers—to have it re-engraved as a copperplate. The first-class workmanship of his engraver has ensured minimum loss of quality; nevertheless there is a slight hardening of the line, and a comparison with an actual Hollar etching, like the one reproduced on page 18, gives some idea of the difference.

The craftsmen-engravers of the nineteenth century became extremely skilful at the job of converting pictures of all kinds into wood engravings, particularly in

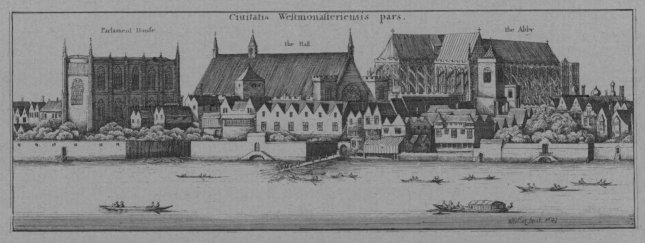

Westminster in 1647. Copper engraving published by J. T. Smith in 1809, based on the etching by Wenceslaus Hollar.

Germany, where the history books of the period are lavishly illustrated with excellently re-engraved plates such as this wood engraving, made about 1870, and based on a broadsheet of 1631. Inevitably, though, much of the original quality was lost. By the end of the nineteenth century, the introduction of photo-mechanical methods was to bring about a revolution in this kind of reproduction, but so long as the subject had to be manually re-drawn, the end-quality depended on the skill—or lack of skill—of the individual craftsman, and at times the results could be horrific.

Gustavus Adolphus of Sweden lands at Peenemunde. Wood engraving from a German history book of about 1870, based on a broadsheet issued in 1631, during the Thirty Years' War.

## Degrees of quality

When assessing an illustration, we must first ask ourselves is 'Is this the form in which the picture originally appeared?' If not, 'What intervening processes have taken place?' And then, 'What is the illustration likely to have lost as a result of those processes?' Reproduced illustrations fall into a hierarchy in order of probable deterioration from the original.

1. Print (off metal, wood, stone) from a drawing made expressly for printing.

2. Print made from a drawing based on a painting or other such original.

3. Print made from a drawing based on a photograph.

4. Print made from a drawing based on a print made by a different process (e.g., wood engraving based on a copperplate, or copperplate based on a woodcut).

5. Print (half-tone or some other modern process) based on any of the foregoing.

We need not assume that the operation of processing an illustration from its original form inevitably means a loss of quality. Certain types of conversion are very easy: thus a woodcut or a silhouette can generally be reproduced with perfect fidelity by line engraving, as is demonstrated by the portrait of Anne Turner (**7a**) or the silhouettes (**33**). Moreover, the craftsman of a later age may well possess greater skill than the original artist; this is undoubtedly the case, for example, with many of the great French engravings of the eighteenth century, where the engraving is frequently a far finer piece of work than the original painting or drawing. But in any case, whether we like them or not, such conversion processes are unavoidable if we are to benefit from illustrations at all. In no other way can the world at large see pictures which either exist only as unique tapestries, paintings or manuscripts, located perhaps in some place not accessible to the general public, or indeed which may have vanished altogether.

Conversion at its most extreme. This copper engraving from Strutt's *Chronicle* of 1777 makes use of illustrations from medieval manuscripts, combining isolated figures and details into a single fairly realistic picture. The plough with its attendant figures comes from the Caedmon MS in the Bodleian Library, Oxford; the harrow from the Bayeux Tapestry; the foreground figures from the Cottonian MS. All have been set against a background showing the Bartlow barrows in Essex.

Of course it is possible to appreciate an illustration without understanding how it was made; nevertheless, its character has been largely determined by the method employed, and a familiarity with technique, however superficial, can deepen appreciation. We have therefore attempted in this section to describe the more relevant graphic processes in terms which are intended for the general reader rather than the artist/craftsman. If experienced readers find much of this chapter embarrassingly basic, we would reply that in order to understand why illustrators over the centuries have elaborated such a complicated variety of solutions to the problem of graphic reproduction, it is essential to understand the true nature of that problem. And to do so, it helps to start with first principles.

But first a word of warning. It is vital to keep in mind that all these varied techniques are only means to ends. If an illustrator chose to use a lithographic technique for his subject, it was not for the sake of making a lithograph as such, but because he believed that this was the most appropriate medium for what he wanted to show (or because it was cheaper, or easier). The self-conscious craftsman, concerned with technique for its own sake, is on the whole a modern phenomenon, and does not concern us here.

This helps to explain why, very often, pictures were produced by methods which make use of more than one technique, or why the techniques were modified to suit the taste of the individual craftsman. The processes as actually employed must often have differed considerably from the basic operations we describe here. What matters is the result.

**Basic principles**

Every illustration starts life as some form of sketch, drawing, painting, photograph or other visual image. If it is to be reproduced in quantity, it must be made suitable for some type of printing process. And all printing, whether of words or of pictures, depends on a single principle: that some parts of a given area are made to leave an impression on a surface, while other parts do not. The contrast between the two parts results in an image.

Most printing methods cannot readily handle large unbroken areas of tone, so the image is generally broken up into lines and/or dots, or the area is mottled in some way. Various devices can be used to make these broken areas suggest unbroken areas. When the dots or lines are crowded closer together, for example, a darker effect is produced; when spaced farther apart, a lighter effect results.

If the original is a sketch or drawing, already made up of lines or dots, it can generally be prepared for reproduction in ways which mean little or no loss of the original quality. Paintings and photographs, on the other hand, which are made up of large areas of light and dark tone, often gradually shading one to another, cannot be reproduced as they are; some equivalent for those areas must be found in terms of lines and dots. The history of illustration has largely been the story of ingenious attempts to produce either an imitation of painting or an acceptable substitute for it. Earlier techniques were limited by the methods of printing available; as these methods have grown progressively more sophisticated, so reproductions have grown progressively more faithful to their originals.

In order to separate the areas required to leave an impression from those that are not, part of the printing surface must be removed. Methods of illustration fall into two main classes, depending on whether everything *except* the image, is cut away, or the image itself is removed and the remaining area left to print. The first method is called *relief* (which implies cutting round the image and leaving it to stand in relief). The second is called *intaglio* (i.e. 'cut in', implying that the image itself is cut into the surface). In addition there are some flat-surface (or 'planographic') processes, such as lithography, which produce the necessary contrast not by cutting, but by exploiting the absorbent/repellant properties of certain substances.

From the reproduction point of view there is a crucial difference between intaglio printing methods and any other. Typematter is so superior when the letters are in relief rather than incised, that the latter is never used except for very special effects. If intaglio illustration is insisted on, it can be included with typematter only if it is printed on a separate sheet, or by a second printing on the same sheet. In either case it adds considerably to the printing cost.

For this reason, until the comparatively recent development of commercially viable offset processes, relief processes were preferred for book illustration wherever cost was a significant factor—which, after about 1820, meant nearly always. Before then, however, for some two centuries, intaglio illustration was used almost exclusively, despite its drawbacks. It is important to remember, when assessing the illustrative processes preferred by each succeeding age, that social and economic factors enter not only into the choice of subject matter but also into the technique by which it is reproduced, and in this way affect its impact on the public. For example, compare a scientific textbook of about 1810, before popular woodengraving (relief and therefore cheap) had been commercially exploited, with a comparable work of 20 or 30 years later, when it had become possible for copiously illustrated literature to be disseminated at prices everyone could afford, speeding and broadening the communication of knowledge in a way which must have contributed significantly to the rate of progress in the sciences and practical arts.

Portrait of Simon Panser, Dutch mathematician: probably early eighteenth century. This woodcut, because it deliberately sets out to do a job normally done by line engraving on metal, provides us with an unusually illuminating opportunity to compare the results of the two techniques. The woodcut gives a rugged boldness, but detail and flexible line are not possible.

Printer's ornament: such cuts as this were used by printers to fill up vacant spaces in their pages. Often they would make their appearance in wholly inappropriate contexts—this one, for example, comes from a treatise on surgery of 1739. But all that mattered to the printer was that, being in relief, these cuts could be inserted among the type-matter whenever a stop-gap was needed.

## 1. Relief Processes

### Woodcut

The woodcut is the oldest known reproducible graphic medium. It is known to have existed in Europe as long ago as 1370, though the first extant dated example is from 1423. The earliest woodcuts were religious pictures, printed on single sheets, probably distributed at pilgrimage centres. In one form or another the woodcut has been used ever since, though its popularity has fluctuated considerably; thus during the seventeenth and eighteenth centuries it was used mostly for broadsheets, advertising bills, ballads, printers' decorations and other popular work.

The characteristics of a woodcut are boldness, contrast, simplicity, ruggedness of line. It lacks the flexibility and subtlety of a metal engraving, but in the hands of a master its range of expression is surprisingly wide.

BASIC TECHNIQUE

1. Drawing is made on a smoothed block of wood (usually pear or alder) which has been whitened with chalk.

2. The white area is cut away with knife, chisel or gouge, leaving only those parts forming the image.

3. Ink is rolled on to the uncut surface of the block.

4. Paper is pressed on to the block, and takes up ink from the outline. (Note that, as with all such processes, this printed image will be reversed, the left hand of the original becoming the right of the print.)

VARIATIONS

Drawing may be made separately on paper which is then gummed on to the block.

In the form of *chiaroscuro*, a key block provides the main outline, while other blocks, applied in separate operations, superimpose areas of shade or colour.

Towards the end of the nineteenth century, wood blocks were replaced by the *electrotype*, a duplicate relief printing plate made by electrolytically depositing metal on to a mould of wax or lead taken from the original wood block; it was then backed with lead alloy. This was considerably less cumbersome to use than the wood block, especially in combination with type-matter.

### Wood Engraving

Wood engraving is essentially the same as woodcutting, but with certain technical variations which produce a somewhat different result. It originated towards the end of the eighteenth century, and its popularity was largely due to Bewick who, though not the inventor of the process, was the first to exploit its full potential.

Even this crude wood engraving from a popular song book of 1845 betrays the influence of Bewick in the treatment of the bushes in the lower right-hand corner.

The technique is the same as that of the woodcut. The difference stems from the fact that while in the woodcut the soft side-grain of the wood is used, in the wood engraving the hard end-grain is used. Furthermore, a harder type of wood (generally box) is employed. This means that finer tools, such as the burin used in metal engraving, can be employed and finer and more subtle work executed.

How accurate this view is of Bewick's workshop is not known—except that Victorian artists generally went to considerable lengths to confirm the truth of their pictures. This illustration itself is an example of wood engraving at its most sophisticated, if not at its finest. It is hard to remember that every mark on this paper was originally made by hand, even though the workman no doubt used various tools to achieve the stippled shading.

In practice it is not always easy to tell a woodcut from a wood engraving. One distinctive feature is the absence or presence of white lines in the picture. It is difficult to achieve these in the soft wood used for the woodcut, but relatively easy in the harder wood of the wood-engraver. Characteristically, therefore, a wood engraving will contain both white lines and black, a woodcut, black lines only.

The wood-cutter can be thought of as treating his block as a white surface, on which black images are created by cutting away the rest; the wood-engraver, on the other hand, treats his block as a black surface, in which 'colour' appears by increasing the number of white lines.

The majority of illustrations in textbooks and popular journals throughout the first two-thirds of the nineteenth century were wood engravings; they are found almost anywhere, in fact, where illustration and text appear together on the same page. Where pictures had to be engraved in a hurry, the picture was drawn on to a number of small blocks bolted together; they were separated so that a number of workmen could work on the individual sections, and were then bolted together again for finishing and printing. This was frequently the case with topical journals such as the *Illustrated London News*, in which block-joins can often be seen.

### Photo-mechanical processes

Towards the end of the nineteenth century, methods were discovered for making line relief blocks mechanically. The picture was first photographed, and the resulting print transferred on to sensitised zinc which, when exposed to acid, was eaten away except where the image had been imposed. Such techniques, known as 'process work', were first introduced commercially in the 1870s, and rapidly became standard practice. By 1900 the electrotype had completely replaced the wood block.

From our point of view, the changeover is not particularly important. Joseph Pennell, an expert on illustration, wrote in 1895: 'To distinguish between a mechanically produced block and one engraved on wood is so difficult that no living expert on the subject would venture an off-hand opinion.' However, it is largely due to this development that we find a generally higher technical quality of printing at the latter end of the nineteenth century, even though the same cannot always be said of the aesthetic results.

A more momentous development came in the 1890s, when it was found that a picture could be broken up mechanically into minute dots by superimposing a screen over it. This not only eliminated the laborious manual operation of converting the picture into lines or dots, it also permitted more subtle effects, such as using larger or smaller dots, by which the effects of dark and shade could be effectively simulated. This was the *half-tone process*, which proved especially suitable first for line-and-wash illustrations and then for photographs; throughout the twentieth century it has been the process chiefly used for the reproduction of illustrations.

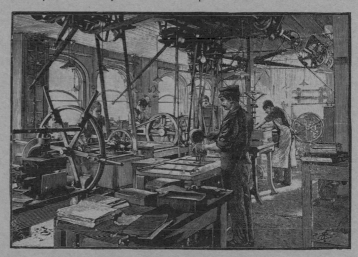

These two views showing work on the illustrations for the *Strand* magazine in 1892 are also, of course, examples of the electrotyping that they illustrate.

Ten years later, a half-tone of a similar subject from *Living London*. By 1903 the half-tone had almost completely replaced the engraving—with a positive gain in credibility, a positive loss in quality.

A disadvantage of the half-tone process is that once a picture has been reduced to dots, it is difficult to reproduce it satisfactorily *again*: at best it can be reproduced, as we have here, as it stands, dots and all. Generally, though, quality is seriously diminished every time it is copied, whereas a line engraving can, with care, be duplicated almost without any loss of quality.

The more serious shortcoming of the half-tone is the fact that, being produced mechanically, it has no respect for the individual qualities of the original. When used by an experienced professional, who can afford to spend time and trouble on it, the results need not be too far below the quality of the original; but too often the time and the trouble are unavailable. By and large it is the half-tone we must blame for the wretchedly low standard of popular illustration we have had to tolerate throughout the past three-quarters of a century.

## 2. Intaglio

*Line Engraving (on metal)*

The limitations of the woodcut encouraged illustrators to seek other ways of re-producing pictures, and this led to the development of line engraving in the mid-fifteenth century. Being costlier than the woodcut, and requiring greater skill, it was not until well into the sixteenth century that the engraving came into general use, having proved its superiority. From then on it continued to be the dominant form of illustration for most purposes, except when, in the nineteenth century, wood returned as the medium for popular low-budget applications.

Copper was almost always used until about 1820; then, as steel became more easily available, its advantages proved more attractive. Though harder to work, steel made possible greater precision and finer detail. Furthermore, a greater number of printings could be taken before the block began to deteriorate. Zinc was used where an especially soft outline was required, but against this benefit lay the drawback that only very few impressions could be taken before the block showed signs of wear.

BASIC TECHNIQUE
1. Plate of copper, zinc or steel, about 2.5 mm thick, is polished as smooth as possible.

2. Design is transferred on to plate. The customary method is for a pencil or crayon drawing to be made on thin paper, which is then damped and pressed on to the plate, leaving a faint grey impression.

3. The plate is cut with a burin, a chisel-like steel tool with a sharp point, which is pushed forward and actually removes the metal in fine slivers. Since the burin can only move forwards, curved lines are made by rotating the plate, which is customarily rested on a round leather cushion. The delicacy of the technique means that not only the outline of a drawing, but also cross-hatching, etc. to represent shading, can be used.

VARIATIONS
Alternatively, plate can be grounded with chalk, and the design traced into the chalk ground through the paper.

In this section we have tried to present a representative selection of illustrations from every period, out of the immense number available. We have also sought to indicate the techniques and styles favoured by each period, as well as the type of subject-matter which most attracted its illustrators. For the most part, therefore, we have kept to the more characteristic types of illustration prevalent at any particular time. But we have included a certain number whose significance has, in our opinion, not been sufficiently valued. To cite just one example: the superb work of John Kay, telling us so much not only about his fellow-citizens of Edinburgh at the end of the eighteenth century but also about the social attitudes of his day, does not seem to have been properly recognised.

We have whenever possible chosen pictures not only for their intrinsic interest but also to make some special point. Thus, while it is revealing to see a picture of siege devices of the mid-seventeenth century, the illustration takes on extra interest when juxtaposed with one of Callot's etchings of the miseries of war.

In general the illustrations are in chronological order: but in such cases as the one just mentioned, we have brought forward later examples for the sake of comparison. Thus we have grouped together eight portraits of Disraeli, taken from different epochs of his career, to show the varieties of popular iconography favoured by the press of his day. Besides, it is often impossible to date a print precisely. For the most part, we have based our chronology on the dates when the original illustrations were made, but in some cases we have broken even this rule in order to make a particular point. Above all, we have tried to bear in mind that, in the terms of reference of this survey, the purpose of the illustration is of prime importance, its technique and attractiveness only secondary. The criterion is, 'What information does the picture communicate?' For this reason we have excluded virtually all pictures illustrating works of fiction, except where they provide us with documentary data—for example, a scene from Fielding's *Joseph Andrews*, which happens to show a typical domestic interior of the later eighteenth century. The original sizes of the illustrations in this section are given in parenthesis—height before width—in millimetres. Every care has been taken to retain as much as possible of the character of the original illustrations. To reflect this both line and half-tone reproduction has been used in the printing of this book by offset lithography.

The further we delve into the world of illustration, the greater the riches we discover. The selection which follows is as representative as we can make it, but for every picture included, there are many which we might have chosen to take its place. This section is not a catalogue; it is a series of signposts, each pointing to greater treasures beyond.

**1a  Metal Mining and Processing**
Woodcut (53 × 85 mm) from a German schoolbook (sixteenth century)

**1b  Witch Calling Down Fiend on Victim**
French woodcut (38 × 63 mm) from *Description des pays septentrionales* (early seventeenth century)

Taken from the earliest days of illustration, this pair of pictures may be used as a warning that communication by illustration has its drawbacks as well as its benefits. The artists of these two woodcuts clearly understood the essential function of illustration. The German artist presents solid information; illustration serves here as the handmaid of education. From the French artist comes fantasy masquerading as fact; illustration, in this case, acts as the accomplice of falsehood. The same child who believes in the existence of the metal worker because he has seen a picture of him, will believe in the witch and the fiend for the same reason. When you turn verbal descriptions into graphic images, you give them an extra dimension of actuality— which means an extra dimension of credibility. Illustration is a vehicle for information, but it can convey falsehood as easily as truth.

*sorciers, léquels sauoyent si bien enchanter & abuser les yeus des regardans, qu'ils changeoyent & déguisoyent tant leurs propres visages, que ceus des autres en vne infinité de sortes, tellement qu'il étoit impossible de les reconnoître. Et n'étoit cela commun seullement aus gens de guerre, & autres sortes d'hommes, mais aussi aus femmes, & jeunes filles, léquelles se sauoyent fort bien faire vn faus visaige de la nuë, & air plus subtil, se contrefaisans auoir quelques fois les palles couleurs, puis de rechef reprenans leur en-bonpoint. Leurs charmes étoyent de si grande vertu, qu'il n'y auoit chose si loing, ne si bien enfermée, ou enchênée, qu'elle ne fissent incontinent trouuer, & venir deuant elles, & la faire voir clerement. Et en vsoyent en céte façon: s'il y a quelqu'vn qui desire sauoir en quel état vit vn sien ami, distant de là cinq cents ou mille lieües, il enuoye querir vn Lappon, ou Finnon bien expert en céte science, auquel il fait present d'vne belle robe de lin ou d'vn arc, le priant qu'il lui face sauoir ce que fait celui duquel il èt en peine, soit ami, ou ennemi, et en quel lieu il èt. Cela fait, ce Finnon entre en vne garde-robe, ou cham-*

**2a Henry VIII and the Papacy**
Anonymous English woodcut (186 × 171 mm) (mid-sixteenth century)

**2b Portrait of Henry VIII**
Engraving (170 × 128 mm) by Cornelis Matsys (1544)

Was Henry VIII essentially the Champion of the Reformed Church and England's hero, as the English artist portrays him, or was he, as seen by a foreign artist who did not feel called upon to flatter, the selfish debauchee consulting no man's interest but his own? As eloquently as any written record—and perhaps more reliably because they cannot be tampered with by later hands—illustrations emphasise the ambivalences of history. No writer of our own day could claim to have justly evaluated Henry's character until his assessment had taken into account Matsys's sardonic portrait.

**3a** Woodcut (107 × 70 mm) from Foxe's *Martyrs*, original edition (1576)

**3b** Copper engraving (170 × 203 mm) from Trappe's edition of the same book (1776)

For about three hundred years, Foxe's *Martyrs* was to be found beside the family Bible in every right-thinking English Protestant home. Edition followed edition; generation after generation read how, though the elder citizens of Colchester were prevented by the authorities from expressing their pity at Laurence's martyrdom, their children swarmed around the fire singing hymns of comfort to the dying man. The comparison between the two versions is informative. The changes in the later version are mainly in the direction of greater verisimilitude—houses are shown in the background, the crowd is larger, the faces are more varied. Curiously, though, the total effect is actually more primitive than that of the earlier woodcut (on which, clearly, the later artist has drawn for his basic material—note, for instance, the position of the martyr chained in his chair). The formal rendering of the flames, the carefully arranged crowd, suggest a set tableau rather than a literal record; indeed, by 1776, this is precisely the purpose Foxe's book was serving. Reading it was an established Sunday afternoon ritual, designed to keep the hatred of Catholicism burning in every true Protestant heart.

Engrav'd
Fox's Book of
Martyrs.

The Martyrdom of John Laurence, at Colchester.

**4a Spanish in Florida, about 1530**
Copper engraving (125 × 163 mm) by Theodore de Bry, from his *Descriptio generalis totius Indiae orientalis et occidentalis* (1596–8)

**4b Spanish in Peru**
Copper engraving (156 × 90 mm) from a history in Latin (seventeenth century)

The adventures of the Spanish Conquistadors in the Americas, which produced perhaps the most extraordinary confrontations between two civilisations in history, were fully documented by contemporary historians. Indeed, the documentation was perhaps more complete than some of the protagonists would have wished: their cruelties were noted as precisely as their courage, their squalid internal squabblings as thoroughly as their fantastic conquests. The German de Bry, then aged over 60, illustrated his classic chronicle with hundreds of plates which help us to visualise this fabulous chapter in the history of mankind.

**5a Lambert Danaeus, Reformer**
Engraving (130×116 mm) by Heinrich de Hondt (about 1599)

**5b Anthonis Mor van Dashorst, Painter**
Engraving (165×127 mm) by Esmé de Boulonois (early seventeenth century)

A technique which is limited to black scratches on a white background would seem inherently incapable of achieving the same depth of expression as an oil painting, with its colour and its smooth grading from one tone to another. Yet these two artists prove that the graphic medium can at its best be a worthy competitor. The earliest engravers in metal tried to imitate the woodcut, but their successors learned to exploit the potential of the harder material and so achieve greater fineness, with the result that their work combines great strength and vividness with a remarkably sophisticated use of dots and lines. When you look at the way de Hondt has built up the face of his subject, for example, you can see how he has used the resources of his medium to the full. It is hard to believe that an oil painting could tell us more about these two men than these two artists have done.

33

**6a  Mermaids**
Anonymous French woodcut (130 × 97 mm) from *Les Images des dieux* (early seventeenth century)

**6b  The Dragon of Babylon**
French engraving (111 × 149 mm) illustrating the *Book of Daniel* (seventeenth century)

Without the illustrator, would we be able to conceive what mermaids and dragons really look like? Thanks to him, we learn that mermaids come in two varieties, some with the fishiness starting at the neck, others at the waist. As for dragons, we find that they are not nearly so alarming as the old descriptions would have us believe; with a bit of care, we feel, Daniel could have made a pet of this creature instead of putting it to death.

**7a Anne Turner**
Anonymous woodcut (125 × 77 mm) (about 1615)

**7b Sir Thomas Overbury**
Engraving (162 × 122 mm) by Reginald Elstracke (about 1615)

The courtier and occasional poet Sir Thomas Overbury became involved in some rather complex political manoeuvrings, as a result of which his enemies contrived to get him imprisoned in the Tower, where they had him poisoned. The principal criminals, including the Countess of Essex, were pardoned, but the smaller fry, including Mrs Turner, an impoverished physician's widow who had been duped into procuring the poison for the deed, were executed in 1615. Both accomplice and victim are portrayed in characteristic fashion. Overbury is shown in the act of writing a poem, every word of which is completely legible. Crude woodcuts of criminals, together with an account, often in ballad form, of their wrongdoings, were commonly sold among the crowd at executions.

**ANNE TURNER,**

EXECUTED AT TYBURN, Nov. 15, 1615;

THE
Portraiture
of Sir
THOMAS
OVERBURY
Knight
ETAT.32

Those Swanlike notes, sung so inspiredly
to thy untimely fall, proves most exact
Lines drawn, from Life; & thy swift Tragedie
Showes but thine owne Soules Prophecie in Act
Thy Name, and Vertues, live To kill thy Mould
was all Imprisonment; and Poyson could.

But thy more heavenly Self from double chaines
sett free (at once), The Body, and the Tower
In that Supreme unpartiall Court remains
w'her nor Ambition, Envy, Lust have power,
Redeem'd from poysonous plotts, from Witches charmes
from Westons & th' Apothecaries harme. W.B.

**8a  The Toothdrawer**
Nineteenth century steel engraving (125 × 182 mm) by Pound from a painting by
Gerrit van Honthorst (about 1620)

**8b  The Chemist**
Nineteenth century steel engraving (133 × 168 mm) by Payne from a painting
by David Teniers (about 1640)

For most of us, the most valuable legacy of the seventeenth-century Flemish painters
is their portrayal of everyday life. Their technique may have been acquired in Italy—
Honthorst's picture could be subtitled 'Homage to Caravaggio'—but their subject-
matter was very much their own choice. The result is an incomparable body of
work, superbly documenting the life and work of peasant and citizen. Had these
artists been deliberately painting a realistic record for posterity, they could hardly
have done their work better. We may question the authenticity of the grouping of
the figures in Honthorst's scene, but we need not doubt that of the implements
in the rack behind the practitioner. We may suspect the somewhat contrived layout
of the chemist's atelier in Teniers' painting, but we owe him thanks for what is
virtually an illustrated catalogue of scientific equipment of the period.

39

**9a Dutch Warships**
Etching (144 × 212 mm) by Remier Zeeman (about 1632)

**9b Stern of a British Man-of-war**
Etched aquatint (253 × 200 mm) by Charles Tomkins (1800) after a drawing by
Willem Vandevelde the Younger (about 1670)

The supremacy of English sea-power was hard pressed during the seventeenth
century, and it was above all the Dutch who disputed it. It is appropriate, therefore,
that Holland should have produced a generation of great marine artists to match
her great sailors. Zeeman handles his authentic detail with such casual confidence
that it never detracts from the freshness of his etching as a whole. Vandevelde, a
Dutch painter who worked in England for a while after the Restoration, was aiming
at a quite different effect: he gives us what is virtually an architect's elevation, but is
clearly aiming at a suggestion of pomp and magnificence, which has been skilfully
enhanced by the engraver. Just how elaborate Tomkins' technique is can be well
appreciated if the section of hull between the right-hand pair of rear gunports is
examined. You will see that the density of the mottling is not merely varied from
one patch to the next, as with the folds in the flag above, but is gently graded with
admirable delicacy. Much of the drawing is very rough-and-ready, but the total
effect remains superb.

DIEV · ET · MON · DROIT

**10a Breaking on the Wheel**
Etching (112 × 254 mm) by Jacques Callot after his own drawing from the series *Les grandes misères de la guerre* (1633)

**10b Siege and Anti-siege Devices**
Anonymous German etching (196 × 134 mm) from a treatise on the art of making war (seventeenth century)

Though warfare in the seventeenth century had yet to make use of the highly professional techniques of today, it had nevertheless been affected by the spirit of progress and by scientific development. Many manuals on warmaking, bristling with diabolical devices for the prosecution of imaginary wars, appeared, chiefly in France and Germany. The military textbook became, indeed, a minor art form— an academic exercise bearing little relation to the actual practice of warmaking. For the reality of war, we have to turn to artists like Callot, especially to his eighteen scenes depicting the miseries of war. Though initially inspired by a particular event (Richelieu's invasion of Lorraine during the Thirty Years' War), they show not specific incidents but generalised indictments which have not lost their impact after three hundred years. The originals are lightly, almost diffidently drawn, as though the artist hesitated to be too precise. But there is no restraint in the force which informs the total composition, and no blow is softened when he comes to expressive detail: the elegant bystanders congregated as for some splendid ceremony, the priest bowing in a parade of sympathy, the executioner's fashionable hat and cape put aside until his morning's work is done.

Callot inv. et fec.

*L'œil toufiours furueillant de la duine Aftrée*
*Bannit entierement le dueil d'vne contrée,*

*Lors que tenant l'Efpeé, et la Balance en main*
*Elle iuge et punit le voleur inhumain,*

*Qui guette les paßans, les meurtrit, et s'en ioüe,*
*Puis luy mefme deuient le ioüet d'vne roüe.*

**11a  Children's Games**
Engraving (203 × 288 mm) by Stefano Scolari of Venice (about 1640)

**11b  The Duke and Duchess of Newcastle and their Family**
Engraving (263 × 159 mm) by Pieter Clouet after Abraham Diepenbeck:
frontispiece to *Nature's Pictures* by Margaret, Duchess of Newcastle (1656)

The Flemish painter Diepenbeck worked in England during the reign of Charles I and
was much employed by the Duke of Newcastle. Among his many pictures is this
delightful family scene which gives us a rare glimpse into the domestic life of the
period. Whether the Duke and Duchess habitually wore laurel wreaths in the
domestic circle is perhaps doubtful, but the homely touch of someone having to
open a window because of the smoking fire is entirely believable. Believable, too,
are the Italian children in Scolari's engraving, playing as happily in their marble
hall as our own young play on the sitting-room carpet. Baby-walker, doll, windmill
toy, ball game, the boy waiting for his little brother to wake up so that he can
continue his game—their behaviour matches that of their modern counterparts,
even if their clothes are so magnificently less practical.

Thus in this Semy-Circle wher they Sitt,
Telling of Tales of pleasure & of witt.
Heer you may read without a Sinn or Crime,
And how more innocently pass your tyme.

**12a The Bastille, Paris**
Etching (110 × 134 mm) by Mathaus Merian from a drawing by himself or one of his assistants (about 1640)

**12b The Castel Sant' Angelo, Rome**
Etching (160 × 128 mm) from Donato's *Rome* (1665)

Mathaus Merian was a Swiss-born engraver and publisher whose many hundreds of topographical pictures provided the seventeenth-century equivalent of post-card views of the cities of Europe. Though executed with little feeling or imagination, they are technically excellent and provide invaluable documentation of the outward appearance of the Europe of his day. Donato's drawing is, by contrast, quite remarkably bad; yet the overall effect of his etchings is most attractive, and the documentary value is incalculable. His plate illustrates the problems the publisher set his printer if he insisted on printing intaglio-engraved plates on the same page as type-matter. This necessitated two printings, with careful registering: note how the pressmark of the engraving almost encroaches on the text. The second printing has made the paper denser within the plate area, giving the effect of a pale grey wash. Technologically naïve, the result is nonetheless aesthetically satisfying, as a result of the inherent good taste of the printer, who has simply juxtaposed picture and text without any fancy business.

**13a** Anonymous etching (163 × 127 mm) (probably late 1630s)

**13b** Anonymous engraving (160 × 125 mm) (probably early 1640s)

Religious intolerance is without peer as an inflamer of passions. Many of our illustrations derive their inspiration from sectarian bigotry. When the two contending sects enlist the help of artists, any information obtained from their work is likely to be about the contenders' preconceptions rather than the subject in hand. For all its naïveté, the equestrian portrait of Sir John Hotham demonstrates that the controversial Parliamentarian deserved to be styled 'Right Worshipfull', until, in the second picture, he is found trampling the sacred books at the devil's bidding and hestitating only between converting St Paul's Cathedral to a stable or leasing it to the Jews. On comparing these illustrations, as they must have been compared in the seventeenth century, it is impossible to tell which, if either, of the artists has portrayed the true Sir John.

**14a  Johann Alphonsus Borello's Submarine Project**
Engraving (70×125 mm) from his *De motu animalium*, reprinted in *Acta eruditorum* (1680)

**14b  Johann Christof Wagenseil's 'Wasser-schild'**
Engraving (173×273 mm) from *Acta eruditorum*, Leipzig (1691)

While the scientist marvelled at the freaks of nature or sought to comprehend her mysteries, he was also compelled to earn his living by applying her laws to practical ends. Scientific journals reported the results with enthusiasm, because they justified the generous financing of scientific research by its royal or noble patrons. Wagenseil's ingenious contrivance was tried out with reasonable success on the Danube at Vienna; the inventor clearly had sufficient faith in his brainchild to venture the life of his human offspring on it. We do not know whether Borello would ever have risked the lives of his children in his submarine boat, since it does not seem ever to have been constructed; however, its clever use of inflatable goatskins, which, when filled with water, sank the vessel, and, when emptied, raised it, was practicable enough to be plagiarised in the *Gentleman's Magazine* of 1749.

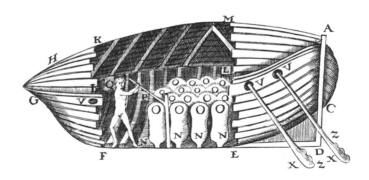

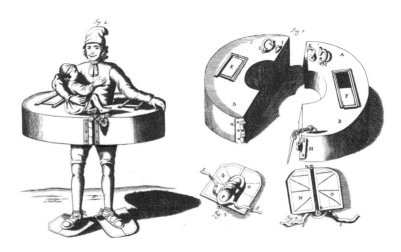

**15a** Engraving (120 × 90 mm) from the *Encyclopaedia Britannica* (1797)

**15b** Engraving (108 × 56 mm) from *Nature Displayed* (an English book, but the engraving was probably lifted from a French original) (1763)

**15c** Engraving (152 × 172 mm) from John Johnstone's *Natural History of Birds* (about 1650)

A revealing comparison, and one which reflects little credit on the compilers of eighteenth-century encyclopaedias, who had the advantage of over a hundred years on Johnstone in discovering what an ostrich really looked like. Johnstone had certainly exaggerated the size of his birds' heads, but, apart from this, his drawings are remarkably accurate for their day. In addition, though all three are charming pictures, only Johnstone seems to have conveyed the feeling that his ostrich is a living creature; the others are hack artists working for the publishers of encyclopaedias, but Johnstone was himself a naturalist.

a  b

c

**16a  Turnip shaped like a Human**
Engraving (155×126 mm) from *Ephemeridum medico-physicarum Germanicarum*
(1680), based on a drawing made in 1628

**16b  The Solar System**
Engraving (232×195 mm) by Jean d'Olivar from the 1701 edition of Fontenelle's
*Entretiens sur la pluralité des mondes* (1886)

The word 'science' did not have its precise modern definition in the seventeenth
century: the scientific journal from which the first of these illustrations was taken
deals not only with early steam engines and comets, but also with freaks animal,
vegetable and mineral. This vegetable freak, whose upper half resembles one of the
ladies of Tahiti encountered by Captain Cook a half-century later, has a surrealistic
charm which makes up for its lack of credibility. Its inclusion in a learned journal
reflects the outlook of an age when scientific curiosity and a belief in marvels co-
existed happily. It was to educate the layman into a proper understanding of the
universe that the French philosopher Bernard de Bovier, Sieur de Fontenelle, wrote
his famous dialogues. Though ridiculed by Voltaire, the book did a useful job in
interesting ordinary people—the second participant in the dialogues was a lady of
fashion—in matters scientific. Pictures such as this must have come as a revelation
to minds not educated to considering the physical nature of the universe. It is a
superb combination of imaginative fancy and scientific fact, and it is also an
excellent piece of engraving, skilfully conveying an almost hypnotic sense of depth.

Aō. 1628. is DESÉ RADŸS DER HEŸDEN
INDEN GARTEN GEWASSEN

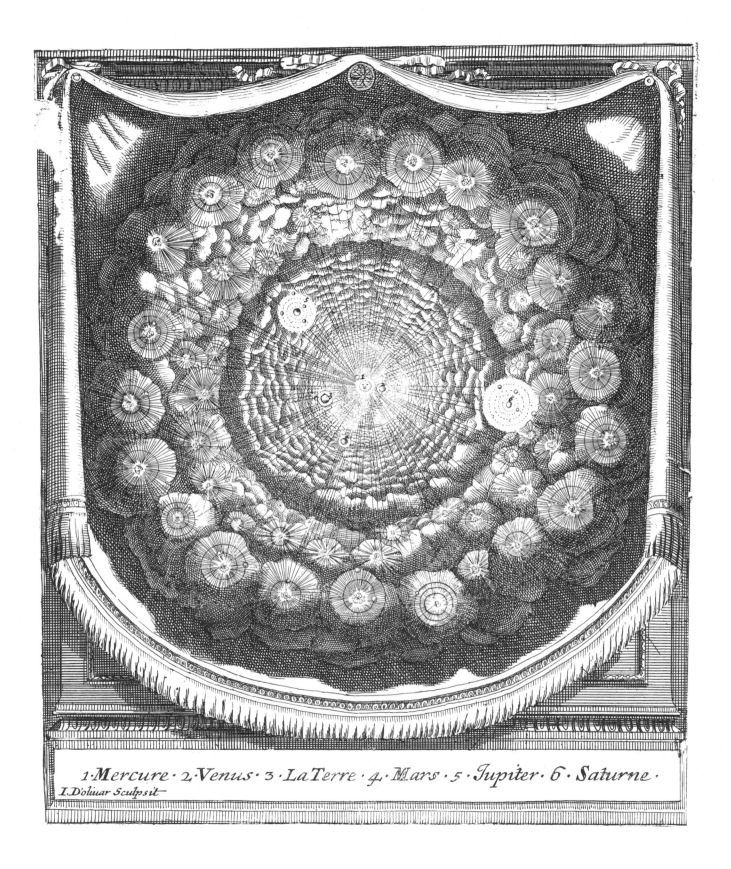

*1.Mercure · 2.Venus · 3 · La Terre · 4 · Mars · 5 · Jupiter · 6 · Saturne ·*

I. D'oliuar Sculpsit

**17a  Baptism Ceremony of the Banians of India**
Engraving (148 × 207 mm) by du Bosc from a drawing by Bernard Picart in his
*Religious Ceremonies of All Nations* (1737)

**17b  Funeral Card for an Undertaker**
Engraving (117 × 166 mm) by J. Ireland from a drawing by Hogarth (1700)

Bernard Picart was a prolific French artist to whom the chroniclers of later ages
owe an enormous debt. His greatest work was the massive seven-volume *Religious
Ceremonies*, a comprehensive study of the world's religions which was lavishly
illustrated with hundreds of engravings of a superb quality. No doubt a fair amount
of allowance must be made for the licence with which Picart interpreted the accounts
given him by travellers, but however questionable their reliability, his drawings
remain a magnificent and often unique record, regularly plundered by later historians, just as he had plundered earlier sources such as de Bry (see **4a**). The
illustrations are often works of considerable artistic merit; indeed, the young
Hogarth learnt his trade by illustrating similar travel books, for which the early
eighteenth century saw a tremendous vogue. His design for an undertaker's funeral
card, a freelance commission, is tackled in much the same spirit, and could well
have been included by Picart as an example of English religious ceremonies.

**18a  Peter the Great**
Engraving (140×89 mm) from the *London Magazine* (1775)

**18b  George I**
Mezzotint (297×253 mm) by John Faber the Younger after a painting
by Stevens (1722)

The mezzotint was a deliberate attempt to reproduce the texture of painting, and within its limitations it succeeded admirably. If a loss of detail and precision can be accepted, together with a somewhat monotonous overall texture, the results can be very attractive. It is not surprising that it was chiefly for portraits that the mezzotint found favour, and this example shows why: the mezzotint avoids the sharp lines and abrupt contrasts of line engraving, replacing them with delicately shaded tones. Nevertheless, the technique remains a compromise, ingenious but never entirely satisfactory. It gives us a splendid and handsome portrait of a gracious king—a view that George I would probably have wished to be presented. At the same time, one would not wish to be deprived of the cruder, simpler view of his contemporary, Peter the Great of Russia—a rare example of royalty portrayed from the rear.

D. Stevens pinx.                                                    John Faber Fecit 1722.

*Georgius I.<sup>mus</sup> D. G. Mag: Brit: Fran: et Hib: Rex: F.D.*

*Brun: et Lunen: Dux S. R. I. Arch: Thesaur: et Princeps Elector &c.*

*Inauguratus 20 die Octobris 1714.*

Sold by John Bowles Print and Map seller at the Black Horse in Cornhill.

57

**19a** Mezzotint (142 × 123 mm) by Charles Spooner (early eighteenth century)

**19b** Steel engraving (142 × 113 mm) (German, early nineteenth century)

**19c** Steel engraving (142 × 113 mm) by Armstrong (early nineteenth century)

Charles Lamb said of Hogarth's pictures 'Other pictures we look at; his prints we read.' Now they provide a unique series of illustrations of daily life in the early eighteenth century, but in Hogarth's time they represented something more: innumerable editions of his engravings were published, drawing solid moral lessons from the careers of rakes, harlots, and idle apprentices. It may, however, be suspected that, then as now, the chief fascination was Hogarth's loving attention to detail, his gift for story-telling. His works were engraved by many different hands in many different styles. Of the three versions shown here, the more finished steel engraving by Armstrong is typical of popular prints and is the version in which most people would be familiar with the picture. The German version is included to show the characteristic light style preferred in that country, making no attempt to simulate the tonal effects of the original. Spooner's mezzotint, probably pirated illegally during Hogarth's lifetime, loses much of the detail, such as the words 'of matrimony' on the girl's prayerbook which indicate that she is dreaming of a husband, but it amply makes up for this by its bolder forms and greater impact. It is also, incidentally, the only one of the three to give the angel the extra joint in his leg, which Hogarth included as a satire on clumsy church art.

a

b

c

59

**20a  Amputation of the Leg**
Engraving (123×146 mm) by J. Mynde from Lawrence Heister's *General System of Surgery* (1739)

**20b  Valentine Greatrakes**
Anonymous engraving (140×116 mm) (about 1700)

If there is one field more than any other in which pictures are more eloquent than words, it is surely surgery. After seeing such illustrations as this amputation scene, the young medical student of the eighteenth century would have no illusions about his chosen profession. From such pictures it is possible to find out how these early operations were carried out, even to the extent of knowing what the protagonists were expected to wear; the courage of both performer and patient is to be admired. The text advises the operator to take a preparatory bowlful of rich gravy, to give him both strength of body and fortitude of mind; nothing is specified for the victim, but no doubt some other beverage was found efficacious. Alternatively, if he chanced to see this picture before the event, he might prefer to entrust himself to the more gentle ministrations of Mr Greatrakes.

**21a The Island of Juan Fernandes**
Engraving (194×455 mm) by Johann Sebastian Muller from Richard Walter's
*Anson's Voyage Round the World* (1741)

**21b The Fortunate Escape of Captain Cook from the Furious Natives of Erramangea**
Engraving (120×177 mm) by Warren from a drawing by Granger for *Bankes'*
*Geography* (1775)

'On the 9th of June, at day-break, we at last discovered the long-wished-for Island
of Juan Fernandes . . .' We have chosen this plate from many fine illustrations of
Anson's epic voyage because it conveys so vividly the excitement of discovery—
the strangeness of the unknown territory, with its prospect of shelter and rest after
the exhaustion of rounding Cape Horn, but also with its possibilities of danger.
That the dangers were real enough is shown by the second picture. Cook's voyages
were particularly well documented not only because of their intrinsic interest but
also because they showed that Britain, although a later starter than Spain and
Portugal, could rank among the great exploring nations. That anyone should bring
back news of Juan Fernandes or Erramangea was interesting enough; that it should
be a Briton, at this period of great national expansion, was cause for special pride.

**22a Pekin Observatory**
Engraving (148×225 mm) by Child for *Salmon's Universal Traveller*, derived
from the travels of Louis Le Comte, who died in 1729 (1752)

**22b Rowley's Orrery**
Engraving (187×230 mm) from *The Universal Magazine* (1749)

Nothing symbolises the Age of Reason better than the orrery—a model made by
man in imitation of the Creation itself. The circling planets are reduced to brass
knobs and elegant dials, the universe is confined within a logical graspable form
and then embellished with decoration, showing that man, no less than God, can
progress beyond the merely practical. That this illustration appears in a magazine
intended for the general public is a reminder that this was an age when a gentleman
—and indeed his wife too—was expected to have at least a casual acquaintance with
the progress of knowledge. Though he might not possess an orrery of his own, he
could familiarise himself with its workings from journals like *The Universal Magazine*; though he might never visit Pekin, he could learn about it from such popular
compendiums as *Salmon's Universal Traveller*, a digest of other people's discoveries.
It is no accident that both titles include the word 'universal', for any work which
promised to scan the whole body of knowledge was sure to appeal at this period
of rapid expansion in all fields of enlightenment.

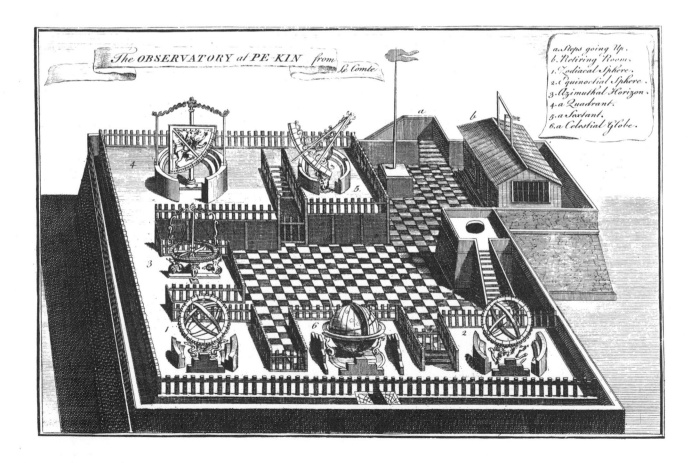

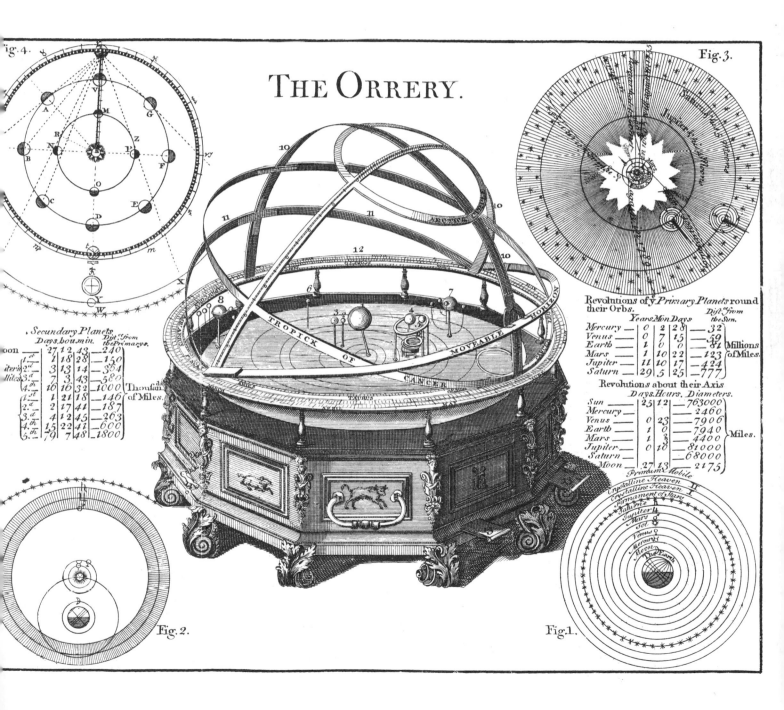

# THE ORRERY.

**23a Elizabeth Canning in the House of Mother Wells**
Anonymous engraving (277 × 234 mm) (1753)

**23b John Williamson Starving His Wife to Death**
Engraving (155 × 97 mm) by Lodge after a drawing by Vangro for the
*New Newgate Calendar* (1818)

Interest in sin and scandal seems to be a permanent characteristic of the human race: they provide the themes of illustrations from the earliest days, forming the subject-matter of all kinds of print from high-quality engravings to popular wood-cuts. The story of the Canning Wonder was one which caught the imagination of all classes of society, and continues to intrigue us today. Many books and articles have been written, yet the mystery of whether Elizabeth Canning was telling the truth has never been completely solved. This fine engraving, published at the height of the controversy and claiming to be drawn from life, clearly takes her part, despite her inability to produce evidence to corroborate a story that, like the house where she claimed to have been confined, was full of holes. There was no room for doubt, however, in the case of John Williamson, a London shoemaker who married a second wife, although she was an idiot, for her money. He locked her in a cupboard, handcuffed and suspended above the floor, until she died. At this point his neighbours rather belatedly informed the authorities, and he was executed at Moorfields in 1767. The *Newgate Calendar*, from which this illustration is taken, was first published in 1774, and appeared in various editions throughout several decades, enlivened with graphic if not especially convincing illustrations.

---

The caption on the picture reads *This young Creature, whose Modesty and General Conduct had always recommended her where known, was kidnapt on the 1st of January last, under Bedlam Wall, by two Ruffians; who, after depriving her of her Sences by the Blows they gave her, forcibly Carried her to the infamous House aforesaid: where, having been first stripp'd by Elizabeth Squires the Gipfy, she was closely shut up in a dismal Room and supported only with stale Crusts and Water, for a whole Month, in order to force her to Prostitution. From these dreadful Circumstances this resolutely-virtuous Creature happily made her Escape, by scratching a way thro' the Wall; whereby she recovered her Liberty and return'd to her Mother's in Rosemary Lane, almost naked, and in a condition too deplorable to be describ'd.*

**24a View of a Port, probably Amsterdam**
Engraving (168×220 mm) by Schleven after Daniel Chodowiecki (about 1770)

**24b View of Potala, Tibet**
Engraving (148×191 mm) by Parr from *Salmon's Universal Traveller* (1752)

The eighteenth-century was the age of the Grand Tour, but this was chiefly for the wealthy or the adventurous. Then as now, most people had to be content with armchair travelling, and were no more likely to visit Amsterdam than Potala. Publishers catered for such a public with pictures which were generally a little (and sometimes a lot) larger than life, doubtless inspiring many a young lad to run away to sea and plant the British flag on yet another unclaimed corner of the world.

The Castle of Putala, the residence of ý Grand Lama.

**25a The Manufacture of Gobelin Tapestries**
Engraving (313 × 203 mm) by Robert Benard from a drawing by Badel for
*L'Encyclopédie* (1751–72)

**25b Benjamin Wilson's Electrical Experiments**
Engraving by James Basire from a drawing by Rooker (about 1760)

The encyclopaedia of Diderot and d'Alembert was one of the great literary, philo-
sophical and scientific monuments of all time—not only the finest product of the
Age of Reason, but a landmark in the history of man's efforts to organise the world
in which he finds himself. In 35 volumes, 12 of them composed of plates, the team
of authors courageously sought to contain all knowledge in one logical framework.
The religious and political views of the *Encyclopédie* were often unorthodox, the
facts were frequently inaccurate, the conclusions sometimes absurd; but there was
never any doubt concerning the value of the work's technological content, which is
perhaps its most enduring aspect. Many of the plates were 'borrowed' from other
sources, a practice which drew well-merited accusations of plagiarism. What is
important is that here, gathered into a single place, is a unique storehouse of
scientific and technical information. For this reason, we have deliberately chosen
a thoroughly matter-of-fact plate, illustrating a single technical detail from a manufacturing process—information which is almost impossible to document from other
sources. Almost equally rare is the glimpse of scientific research in progress, as
recorded in Basire's fine engraving. All too often one can only find documentation
of the outcome of research; here, for once, is modern science in the making.

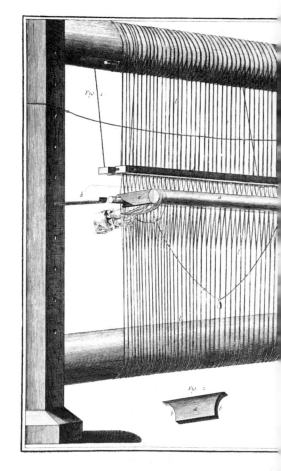

**26a  Justice of the Peace with Friend**
Engraving (117 × 197 mm) by Sanders after a drawing by John Collier (about 1772)

**26b  The Houndsditch Macaroni**
Etching (216 × 152 mm) by Bretherton from a drawing by Bunbury (1772)

Probably no artist portrays more effectively than Collier the pervasive lechery of the eighteenth century. He was a Lancashire schoolteacher given to designing grotesque figures for the walls of taprooms, an unusual sideline for a man of his profession. In the 1770s he published under his *nom de plume* of 'Tim Bobbin' a series of drawings of his favourite subjects; their force is sufficient to make up for the deficiencies of his draughtsmanship. His contemporary, Henry William Bunbury, was also an educated man; perhaps it was during his time at Cambridge that he discovered his talent for caricature. Like many a comic artist before and since, he capitalised on the disparities which inevitably occur in a period of rapid social change. The term 'macaroni' had originally been applied to men of fashion who had picked up Italianate habits in the course of the Grand Tour; subsequently it became applied to any dandy such as this vulgar fellow from the City, who sets out to ape his betters in powdered wig, three-cornered hat, sword and all.

*The caption on the picture reads*
So have I seen a Justice on the bench
Brow-beat and scold a poor deluded wench,
Who when at home with Molly snugly plays,
Tickles her tuft, and laces on her stays.

**27a General Burgoyne and the Indians in 1777**
Copper engraving (133×190 mm) by J. Taylor from an original by Woodruff,
for Smollett and Hume's *History of England* (1804 edition)

**27b Decatur at Tripoli in 1804**
Steel engraving (184×142 mm) after the original painting by Chappel (about 1860).

Graphic treatment of historical events can be most ineffective: by reducing them
to a series of formal tableaux, it removes them from reality and locates them in a
land of fancy. If this is how George III and his ministers pictured the American
problem, it is no wonder that they lost the Colonies. Aesthetically, of course, the
picture is most agreeable: notice how the thoroughbred horse, not altogether
pleased that his noble master should fraternise with lesser breeds, strikes an elegant
attitude while turning his face disdainfully away. Decatur's conflict at Tripoli has
also been reduced to a set-piece, looking as if a war artist had asked the protagonists
to hold their positions so that he could catch their attitudes in his sketch-book.
As a piece of engraving, it is a magnificent example from the period when American
engravers led the world: the rendering of texture—the clothes, the grain of the deck
—is executed with a remarkable skill which is rarely found in European engraving
of the period, but which seems to have come easily to the Americans.

**28a  A Mother Abbess of the Last class**
Engraving (124×97 mm) by Matthew Darly (1773)

**28b  The Endless Knot of Love**
Engraving (190×177 mm) by Francesco Bartolozzi from his own drawing (late eighteenth century)

Darly's delightful series portraying 'ladies of the town' provides a unique record of what might be expected of a *fille de joie* in the 1770s. It is only fair to say that, in choosing an example, we have gone to the bottom of the pile: compared with this soiled dove, the Nun of the First Class, for instance, is all glorious without, whatever she may have been like within. Our Abbess is not helped by her moustache or her unaffected hair style; and though we may do her the kindness of supposing that her patches are for adornment rather than relics of the pox, we shudder to think what else one might discover before the night was out. A complete contrast is provided by Bartolozzi's forget-me-not; this is hardly a characteristic example of his work (see, rather, **34b**), but a charming piece of nonsense to set beside the Mother Abbess.

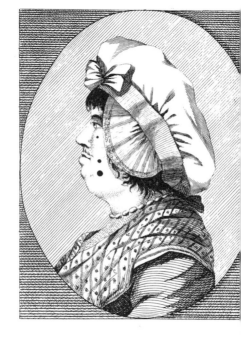

FORGET
ME
NOT

THE ENDLESS KNOT OF

LOVE

F. Bartolozzi R.A. Inv. Delt. et Sculpt.

**29a Garrick and Miss Younge as Tancred and Sigismunda**
Engraved (135 × 178 mm) by Thornthwaite after Roberts for Bell's *British Theatre* (1776)

**29b Tranquil Joy** (105 × 95 mm)
**29c Devotion** (110 × 75 mm)
Engravings from Henry Siddons' *Practical Illustrations of Rhetorical Gesture and Action* (1807)

'I'll come no more behind your scenes, David', Samuel Johnson told his friend Garrick, 'for the silk stockings and white bosoms of your actresses excite my amorous propensities.' Spectacular costume was necessary to match the spectacular histrionics of the period, when the personality of the individual actors counted for far more than the play itself, which was often little more than a vehicle for a Garrick or a Mrs Siddons. The stage-struck amateur who aspired to follow in their footsteps could pick up the tricks of the trade from Henry Siddons' comprehensive handbook. He would also learn that Miss Younge (**29a**) is endeavouring, in her gorgeous dress, to register alarm, while her companion is expressing calm re-assurance with every muscle, and particularly with the third and fourth fingers of his left hand.

b

a

c

**30a Joseph Andrews and Lady Booby**
Engraving (160×102 mm) by Heath from a drawing by Dodd for Fielding's
*Joseph Andrews* (1779)

**30b Lotte**
Engraving (210×176 mm) in the crayon manner by C. W. White from a drawing
by Bunbury for Goethe's *Werther* (1782)

In this book we have deliberately chosen not to deal with illustrations to fiction
in their own right; but occasionally such pictures can have a documentary value
which is relevant to our purpose. Charlotte, for instance, the heroine of Goethe's
extremely successful first novel, *The Sorrows of Young Werther*, was the model for
every sensitive female in Europe and America. In consequence Bunbury's exquisite
drawing has a unique value, since it shows all that the young lady of the period
aspired to be. Again, the spectacle of the lady of the house trying to seduce her
manservant may or may not have been an everyday occurrence, but we may be
confident that the lady and her servant are dressed according to their social status
and the room correctly furnished. Dodd's illustration thus gives us a useful
reference for such matters.

The crayon manner used by White for the Lotte picture is a variant of etching;
in it the texture of crayon lines is imitated with various tools and helped out by
stippling. It was one of several sophisticated techniques designed to reproduce
artist's techniques more faithfully; the effect is very close to that of a lithograph,
so it is not surprising that when lithography was perfected, the crayon manner
disappeared.

**31a  La Petite Toilette**
Engraving (217 × 179 mm) by Pierre Antoine Martini after a drawing by
Moreau le Jeune, from his *Le Monument du Costume* (about 1780)

**31b  Le Vrai Bonheur**
Engraving (215 × 179 mm) by J. B. Simonet after Moreau le Jeune (about 1780)

Few societies can have been recorded in pictures so splendidly as the aristocratic
world of the French eighteenth century. A mass of superb plates, probably the
finest examples of the engraver's art, perfectly reflect the life of the period. These
*estampes galantes* capture a frivolous, pleasure-seeking, idle society. If we can hold
our social consciences in check for a moment, we must surely admire the charm
both of that way of life, and of the pictures which mirror it. Moreau gives us as
accurate a picture as one could hope to find of domestic life in the household of a
young aristocrat; a decade later this nobleman's world was to collapse, and he, in
all probability, would lose the head which is being so carefully tended by his hair-
dresser. Perhaps, like some of his contemporaries, he had doubts from time to
time about his way of life, perhaps he pretended to sigh for the 'true happiness'
depicted in our second illustration. But frankly, he does not look particularly
unhappy as he comments on his new frock-coat, and his idea of happiness more
probably takes the form of the happenings in the two pictures over the mantelpiece
which have to be curtained off from vulgar eyes.

**32a  The Duchess of Devonshire Electioneering for Fox**
Hand-coloured copper engraving (212×320 mm) by Thomas Rowlandson (1784)

**32b  Leaving off Powder**
Hand-coloured etching (231×345 mm) by James Gillray (1795)

At the Westminster election of 1784 the Duchess of Devonshire and other Whig ladies were alleged to have traded kisses for votes; here the Duchess is shown canvassing a butcher, encouraged in her noble efforts by a lady of the town, while Fox himself orates in the background. It is a characteristic example of the work which established Rowlandson as the most devastating caricaturist of his day—at least until James Gillray. Gillray started his career as a strolling player and ended it as a lunatic. Between these extremes he poured out a flow of satirical drawings which made him the most popular printmaker of his age—the appearance of a new Gillray was an event for which the print-shops were besieged by collectors. In this print he satirises Pitt's tax on hair powder, a piece of legislation which was largely instrumental in ending the fashion of wearing wigs.

**33a Edward Gibbon**
Engraving (120×95 mm) from a cut-out paper silhouette

**33b Jane Taylor, Author of 'Twinkle, Twinkle Little Star', etc.**
Engraving (60×50 mm) from a silhouette drawn in ink

**33c Lavater's Silhouette-Making Machine**
Wood engraving (168×152 mm) from *Le Magasin Pittoresque* (1865)

**33d Nelson**
Engraving (120×75 mm) from a silhouette probably drawn in black crayon

**33e The Empress Maria Theresa's Last Day, 1780**
Engraving (105×140 mm) containing silhouette portraits

b

Although profile art has been used in one form or another from the earliest civilisations, the silhouette as a popular form of portraiture enjoyed its chief vogue between 1750 and 1850. Its use was for the most part limited to family keepsakes, but it occasionally happens that no portrait other than a silhouette survives of some individuals: Keats' friend, Fanny Brawne, is one example. At the height of the vogue one could have one's silhouette taken by artists at street corners, in the Thames Tunnel, on Brighton Pier, or simply by one's nearest and dearest at home, which explains why few silhouettes were signed by their creators. For the upper classes silhouettes were an amusing toy, but for the poorer classes they were a means of having one's portrait taken without undue expense, and their popularity lasted until the emergence of the street photographer.

a

c

d

e

**34a Danet's Hall, Leicestershire**
Engraving (130 × 184 mm) by Walker after a drawing by Throsby for his set of
*Views of Leicestershire* (1789)

**34b Family Scene in Summer**
Engraving (128 × 162 mm) by Bartolozzi after a painting by William Hamilton,
illustrating Thomson's *Seasons* (1793)

The first of these pictures was published four months after the Fall of the Bastille:
the second, four months after the execution of Louis XVI. There is significance in
the fact that the gentlemanly life depicted here, unlike that shown in **31a**, is hardly
one which would inspire the lower classes to revolution. Danet's Hall is no lordly
chateau, dominating the village and its inhabitants. The aristocrat in the family
scene, far from indulging himself in the excesses his wealth and position might allow,
exhibits on a slightly grander scale the domestic virtues which all citizens were
exhorted to respect. These two pictures present the epitome of all that the eighteenth-
century English gentleman admired and respected; they help to explain why there
was no English Revolution in 1789, and how George III avoided the fate which
befell Louis XVI.

**35a The Flying Philosopher**
Unidentified engraving (70×90 mm) (late eighteenth century)

**35b Major Mony's Perilous Situation**
Engraving (100×166 mm) by Owen from a drawing by Thurston for
*The Gallery of Nature and Art* (1785)

Men had always dreamed of flying. When they tried to turn their dream into fact, they generally chose some shape which imitated that of a bird, as our Flying Philosopher demonstrates. But the first successful aerial voyage was by balloon, and, though birdmen have continued to make their abortive and often fatal ventures at intervals ever since, the balloon dominated the first century of aviation. Inevitably there were accidents, but in fact they were surprisingly few and not necessarily fatal. Major Mony was particularly lucky to survive, since a Dutch fishing-boat, the vessel which happened to be closest to him after his misadventure, refused to pick him up. This refusal attracted the comment that it was the only occasion on which a Dutchman had been reluctant to pick up 'money'.

---

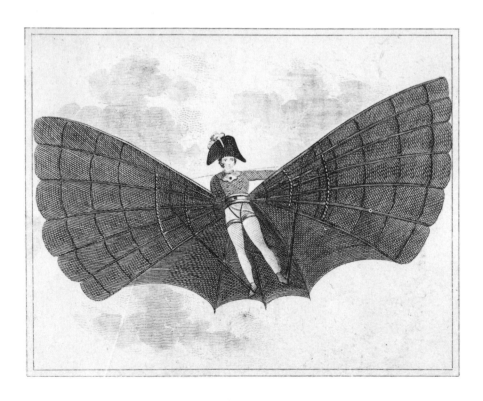

**36a  Self-Portrait with Cat** (96×96 mm)

**36b  Deacon Brodie and George Smith** (168×114 mm)

**36c  Portrait of Miss Luckie Smith** (176×100 mm)

Etchings by John Kay from his own drawings (1786, 1788, 1795)

John Kay, barber turned miniaturist, portrayed his Edinburgh contemporaries with a unique blend of charm and wit, allied to a real affection for his subjects. Clearly he must have liked Miss Luckie Smith, to have portrayed her so elegantly while gently satirising her haughty airs. He must also have liked Deacon Brodie, the highly respectable citizen who dabbled in amateur burglary, for both he and his accomplice are drawn with an insight which sympathises rather than passes judgment. As for Kay's self-portrait, how could he hope to find another artist capable of treating the subject with such a blend of affection and mockery? His most respectful portraits are never without a dash of irony, yet his most extravagant satire is never bitter. And all is done with so casual a skill, such simple sureness of touch, that he can introduce a surrealistic cock and dog into his picture of Brodie as though they were just what you would expect to see there.

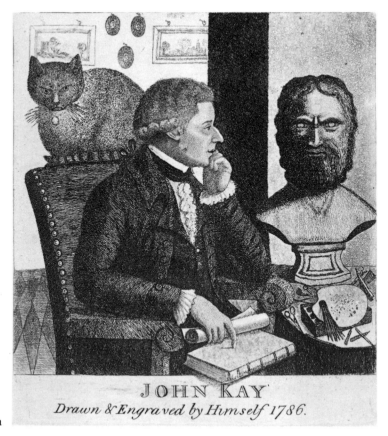

a

b

c

**37a Pattereras**
Engraving (185 × 132 mm) by S. Hooper (1788)

**37b Gunnery**
Engravings (229 × 180 mm) by Bell from the *Encyclopaedia Britannica* (1797)

Here are two ways of conveying a mass of useful information. Bell displays all his goods as if he were the owner of a supermarket—here it is, take your pick. In comparison with this pleasant but limited approach Hooper goes farther and tries harder. In one admirably composed illustration he shows what the pattereras looks like, how to mount it, how to load it, how to fire it and, in the background, how it can be used to defend or attack a vessel.

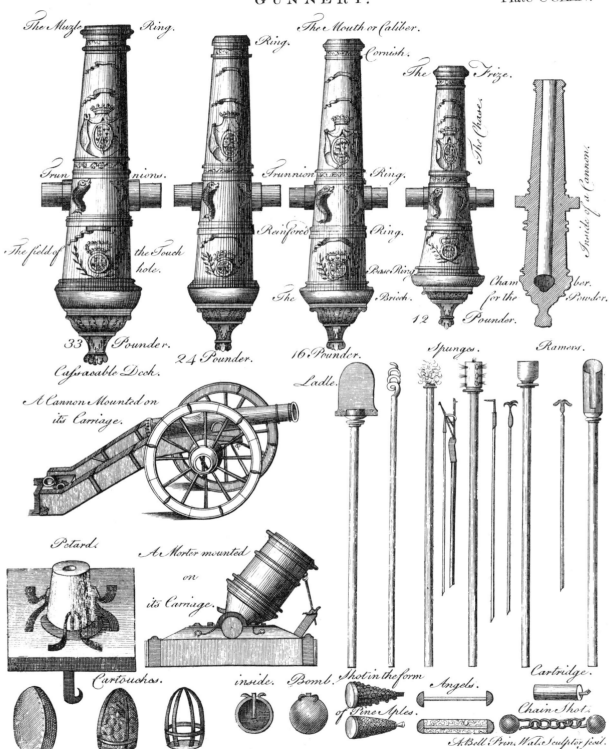

The Muzle    Ring.    The Mouth or Caliber.

Ring.    Cornish.    The    Frize.

Trun    nions.    Trunnion    Ring.    The Chase.

Reinforc'd    Ring.

The field of    the Touch    Base Ring.    Cham    ber.
hole.    The    Briech.    for the    Powder.

Inside of a Cannon.

33 Pounder.    24 Pounder.    16 Pounder.    12 Pounder.

Cassacable Deck.    Spunges.    Ramers.

A Cannon Mounted on    Ladle.
its Carriage.

Petard.    A Morter mounted
on
its Carriage.

Cartouches.    inside.    Bomb.    Shot in the form    Angels.    Cartridge.
of Pine Aples.    Chain Shot.

A. Bell Prin. Wal. Sculptor fecit.

**38a Tailpiece** (50 × 80 mm)

**38b Head of Hippopotamus** (75 × 80 mm)

**38c Squirrel** (45 × 70 mm)
Wood engravings from *The History of Quadrupeds* (1790)

**38d Bill for Inn at Ferry Hill**
Wood engraving (148 × 88 mm)

b

Throughout the seventeenth and eighteenth centuries, no artist took wood engraving seriously. When the author of a mathematical book asked his printer to include some illustrations, he took it for granted they would be done on copper. But the printer pointed out that if the illustrations were cut on wood, they could be printed along with the text—cheaper and more practical for such a book. The author agreed, and the printer's apprentice, Thomas Bewick, was commissioned to do the cuts. So successful were they that he was advised to continue as a wood engraver, advice which he fortunately took. His first major triumph was the *History of Quadrupeds*, from which three of our illustrations are taken. The delicacy with which the squirrel is rendered, the vigour of the hippopotamus, demonstrates the variety of which the wood engraving was capable in Bewick's hands. It is probably true to say that he affected the art of illustration more than any other single craftsman. He prepared the way for the rapid spread of wood engraving in the early nineteenth century, a spread which resulted in the production first of less costly illustrated books and then of popular illustrated periodicals. He had many imitators, some of whose work was nearly as good as his own; but what he accomplished was a one-man revolution almost without parallel in the history of art. The remainder of this volume would look very different if Bewick had not listened to his employer's advice.

a

Sam.ᵈ BEARDSLEY,

FERRY-HILL.

L S

Breakfast

Dinner

Tea & Coffee

Supper

Wine

Brandy

Rum

Gin

Cyder

Beer & Porter

Hay & Corn

Servants Eating

d

## THE SQUIRREL.

*(Sciurus Vulgaris*, Lin.—*L'Ecureuil*, Buff.)

THIS beautiful little animal is equally admirable for the neatness and elegance of its formation, as for its liveliness and activity. Its disposition is gentle and harmless. Though naturally wild, it is soon familiarised to confinement and restraint; and though excessively timid, it is easily taught to receive with freedom the most familiar caresses from the hand that feeds it.

It usually lives in woods, and makes its nest of moss or dry leaves in the hollows of trees. It seldom descends upon the ground, but leaps from tree to tree with great agility.

Its food consists of fruits, almonds, nuts, acorns, &c.; of which it accumulates great stores for winter provision, and secures them carefully near its nest. In the summer it feeds on buds and young shoots, and is particularly fond of the cones of the fir and pine trees.

c

**39a Court dress for 1773**
Engraving (92 × 62 mm) of that date

**39b The Miss-conceptions**
Engraving (88 × 135 mm) from the *Carlton House Magazine* (1793)

**39c Robe du Matin**
Hand-coloured plate (157 × 92 mm) from *Costume Parisien* (1816)

**39d Gentlemen's Outdoor and Indoor Dress**
Hand-coloured plate (165 × 158 mm) from *Petit courrier des dames* (1839)

The fashion plate was a product of the lady's magazine, a medium which established itself towards the end of the eighteenth century as the arbiter of taste and which has maintained this position with almost consistent success up to our own day. Then as now, the aim was to show less affluent women what the well-dressed lady was wearing, particularly in Paris. We must of course be on our guard against supposing that every female of the day dressed *à la mode*. But with this proviso, these plates provide magnificent references for costume as well as throwing interesting sidelights on behaviour and styles in furniture and decoration. The magazines for gentlemen on occasion poke fun at the extremes of female fashion, as in this plate from the *Carlton House Magazine*, mocking a current style of dress which suggested that its wearer was in an interesting condition. However, a man who himself aspired to dress fashionably could turn to his lady's journal and see what was expected of him. This print of 1839 not only tells him where to purchase the clothes but also where to have his hair so becomingly styled.

a

b

c

(1614.)

d

**40a  Napoleon Bonaparte**
Popular French contemporary engraving (188 × 170 mm)

**40b  Napoleon Playing Whist with English Children on St Helena**
Wood engraving (90 × 115 mm) by Charlet from Las Cases' *La Memoriale de Ste Helene* (1822)

**40c  Captain Kelly's Gallantry at Waterloo**
Engraving (140 × 175 mm) by Mitan from a drawing by Captain Jones for Kelly's *The Memorable Battle of Waterloo* (1816)

**40d  La Religion Triomphante**
Engraving (200 × 170 mm) (about 1800)

b

Has any phenomenon ever attracted such a variety of illustration as Napoleon? There are countless portraits—some adulatory, some hostile, but all fascinated, and innumerable battle scenes—French, German and British victories magnificently depicted by French, German and British artists. Even if all these pictures are discounted, those remaining possess a richness and variety hard to match elsewhere. Here are four examples of such work. The popular print illustrates the iconography of the people which is so easily ignored: this Napoleon, not that of the portraits at Versailles or Les Invalides, is the Napoleon so admired, execrated or feared by his contemporaries. The religious allegory is included for its naïveté; it is hard to believe that at so late a date in history angels and devils could be shown contending for the Cross, with Napoleon, by the simple act of attending mass at Notre Dame, scattering the forces of darkness. The gallant Captain Kelly symbolises the many individuals caught up in the great Napoleonic story; this is, for once, a battle picture in which the chiefs of staff do not take the centre of the stage. Finally, a reminder that, despite all the myth-making, Napoleon was a human being, liable to be lured into playing card games with schoolgirls. Napoleon does not usually win affection, but here for once he wins a little sympathy as well as admiration.

a

c

d

**41a  Greek Military Movements**
Engraving (105×175 mm) by W. and D. Lizars for Potter's *Antiquities
of Greece* (1813)

**41b  The Revenge of Chiomare**
Engraving (92×128 mm) by Baquoy after S. de Mirys for *Histoire de la République
Romaine* (1810)

Mirys' magnificent series comprises 181 highly finished plates: he must have set
out on his task when republican fervour was at its fiercest. Looking for an historical
precedent for France's great popular movement, he found natural inspiration in the
great age of pre-Imperial Rome. Unfortunately, long before he reached the end of
his work, France too had become an empire, and republican virtues had been forgotten. However, appreciation of the moral principles embodied in his pictures
should not have been too greatly impaired by a change of government: even an
imperialist can admire the noble conduct of Chiomare, a Gaulish lady who, dis-
honoured by a centurion from the Roman army of occupation, slew her ravisher
and flung his head at her husband's feet. The illustration is suitably noble in the
classical style, fashionable in this period, and superbly engraved with a magnificent
technique developed before the Revolution. Incidentally, the text is also engraved,
which of course entailed the formidable task of working in reverse. While the
French turned to the past for patriotic inspiration, the English were interested in
the practical information offered by history. This Lizars plate does precisely what
an illustration should do: it makes plain what would otherwise be an almost un-
communicable description of a complex operation. The intricate movement has
been rendered with an admirable simplicity which, incidentally, makes a very early
use of isometric figures.

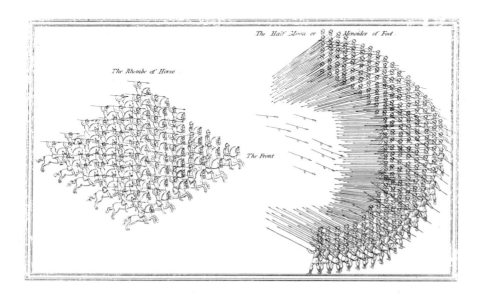

S. de Mirys. Inv. et Del.

Baquoy. Sculp.

## ACTION EXTRAORDINAIRE D'UNE GAULOISE.
### An de Rome 563.

Les Romains avaient à se plaindre des Etoliens et des Galates ou Gaulois Grecs qui s'étaient déclarés contre eux en faveur d'Antiochus. Après la défaite de ce Prince, les Consuls Fulvius et Manlius, furent chargés de punir ces deux Peuples, qui subirent bientôt le joug du vainqueur.

Parmi les prisonniers faits sur les Gallo-Grecs, était une Femme nommée Chiomare, mariée à un des principaux Gaulois qui s'appelait Ortiagon. Elle avait été mise sous la garde d'un Centurion aussi avide d'argent qu'effréné dans ses desirs. Ce malheureux après avoir fait violence à une femme que sa captivité rendait encore plus respectable, lui promit de la renvoyer en liberté, moyennant une forte somme d'argent. On convint du lieu ou se ferait l'échange. Dès la nuit suivante deux parens de l'infortunée Gauloise se trouverent au rendez-vous, ou le Centurion amena sa prisonnière. Tandis qu'il était occupé à peser l'or qu'on avait apporté pour la rançon, elle saisit une épée, tue l'Officier Romain, lui coupe la tête et l'emporte enveloppée dans les plis de sa robe. Arrivée près de son époux, elle jette à ses pieds cette tête sanglante. Ortiagon effrayé d'un tel spectacle, lui demande la cause d'un événement aussi étrange. Le visage couvert d'une subite rougeur et enflammée en même tems d'une fiere indignation, Chiomare avoue à son mari l'outrage qu'elle avait reçu et la vengeance qu'elle en avait tirée.

**42a  Esther Hammerton, Sexton**
Engraving (160×104 mm) from *Wonderful Characters* (1813)

**42b  General Tom Thumb**
Lithographed poster (252×223 mm) by G. Webb & Co. (1849)

Books about freaks and eccentrics have always found a ready market; no doubt psychologists can explain why. Esther Hammerton appears in many of the collections made during the eighteenth and nineteenth centuries. Born in 1711, a grave-digger's daughter, she was involved in the accident when a chapel collapsed, killing her father. She was then aged 19, and robust enough, so she took on her father's job. She studiously avoided every sort of female employment, but was particularly partial to such manly sports as cricket, football, bull-baiting and skating. She preferred the company of men to that of women, but preserved her moral character wholly unimpeached. General Tom Thumb is better remembered than Esther Hammerton today, and was better known than her in his own time too, thanks to the performances he gave up and down the country. The Crowned Heads of the World had seen him; 3,000,000 lesser mortals had seen him; and now, on Monday 24 August, 1849, at three separate performances, the sensation-hungry townsfolk of Ryde were to see him!

Under the distinguished Patronage of
HER MAJESTY, PRINCE ALBERT, THE QUEEN DOWAGER,
THE KING AND QUEEN OF THE FRENCH, THE KING AND
QUEEN OF THE BELGIANS, THE EMPEROR OF RUSSIA, THE
QUEENS OF SPAIN, THE ROYAL FAMILIES AND NOBILITY OF
ENGLAND, FRANCE, BELGIUM AND SPAIN,
and visited during the last two years by

MORE THAN 3,000,000 PERSONS.

# GEN.ᴸ TOM THUMB

The American Man in Miniature, 14 years of Age, 25 inches
high, and weighs only 15 pounds, will hold his Farewell Levees

POSITIVELY FOR *One* DAY ONLY
IN THE *Town Hall Ryde*
On *Monday Aug.ᵗ 24*
previous to his Final Departure for America.

The little General will appear in his various extra-
ordinary Performances and Costumes, including
Songs, Dances, Ancient Statues, the Napoleon and
Highland Costumes, Citizens Dress, &c. &c.

HOURS OF EXHIBITION
*12 to 2, 3 to 5, 7 to 9*

ADMISSION ONE SHILLING
CHILDREN UNDER TEN YEARS OF AGE HALF PRICE

The General's Miniature Equipage will promenade the Streets
during                                        the day.

THE MAGNIFICENT PRESENTS            RECEIVED FROM THE FIRST
CROWNED HEADS IN THE                WORLD WILL BE EXHIBITED.

G. Webb & Cᵒ Litho               Farringdon St. Lond.ⁿ

**43a Ferreting**
Aquatint (120×188 mm), artist unknown (about 1820)

**43b Dick Turpin Bilks the Toll at Hornsey**
Lithograph (119×200 mm) by W. Clerk from *Turpin's Ride to York* (anon.) (1839)

The aquatint was perfectly suited for the reproduction of water-colour paintings, which were much in vogue about this period: hence its name, for water has no other connection with the technique. It was able to reproduce areas of flat tone in a way which avoided the rather overpowering effect of the mezzotint, and would combine more happily with the pure line needed for such details as the net in **43a** (Line has also been used in other parts of the picture, such as the outline to the boys' clothes, but it could have been dispensed with.) This is the aquatint at its most successful, giving a softness and spontaneity that a line engraving or a woodcut rarely affords. Where expressiveness is more important than precise detail, the lithograph offers another valuable alternative. The soft outlines and strong shaded areas give an excitement to this dramatic scene which few engravings could hope to equal. Like the ferreting scene, Clerk's lithograph is no work of art, but it, too, makes good use of an alternative technique.

**44a** Steel engraving (218×136 mm) by Lowenstam after a drawing by Maclise (about 1826)

**44b** Steel engraving (120×100 mm) after a drawing by the Count d'Orsay (1837)

**44c** Steel engraving (230×180 mm) by Robinson after a painting by Chalon (about 1840)

**44d** Etching (85×90 mm) by Magrath (1853)

**44e** Coloured lithograph (310×183 mm) by 'Ape' from *Vanity Fair* (1869)

**44f** Steel engraving (135×112 mm) after a photograph by Mayall (1860s)

**44g** Lithograph (235×200 mm) presented with the *Glasgow News* (1873)

**44h** Wood engraving (150×225 mm) from the *Illustrated London News* (1881)

It is enlightening to compare the varieties of technique employed to present the image of a public figure throughout his life. In the first plate Disraeli is the young man-about-town pure and simple, successful author of a brilliant first novel, all set for a fashionable career; Maclise's elegant drawing could not be more appropriate. D'Orsay still shows us a dandy, but a dandy who has now discovered a sense of purpose; after three attempts to enter Parliament, he has at last succeeded. By the date of Chalon's portrait he is properly embarked on his political career, though still a little flamboyant for the British public. Magrath's portrait uses etching to suggest the on-the-spot sketch, giving us the established statesman, completely at home in the House—an impression confirmed by the fact that he is now considered worthy of a cartoon in *Vanity Fair*. In the 1870s come further confirmations of success: he sits, as did all his great contemporaries, for Mayall's definitive photograph, and newspapers give away portraits of him to mark such special occasions as his installation as Lord Rector of Glasgow University. Finally, in the last year of his life, with his career drawing to a close, the journals wax sentimental, and show the great man at home, his dog at his feet, his battles over.

a

b

c

d

h

f

g

**45a Thomas Cox Savory's Shop**
Lithograph (135 × 114 mm) on zinc by A. R. Grieve (late 1830s)

**45b St Bride's Avenue, Fleet Street**
Steel engraving (141 × 93 mm) by Tingle after a drawing by Thomas Shepherd for
his *Metropolitan Improvements* (1829)

The London of about 1830 has been uniquely preserved in one of the finest topographical collections ever made—Shepherd's *Metropolitan Improvements*. Unlike so
many artists, he shows London as it really was, with sufficient precision to satisfy
a student of architecture, but with sufficient animation in the form of passers-by
and traffic to convince us that we are seeing a real, not an idealised, London.
Shepherd uses the steel engraving with an expertise which exploits not only its
capacity for detail (note the careful precision with which he draws his buildings)
but also its delicacy (note the beautiful rendering of the cloudy sky). In all probability,
it was Shepherd's accomplishment which inspired Grieve's fine lithographic advertisement for Mr Savory's establishment: the detail is only fractionally less precise,
while the rendering of textures, the brickwork and the cobbles, for instance, is
considerably more effective. As to the effectiveness of the drawing as an advertisement, observe the delicacy with which the artist indicates the accessibility of his
client's premises, whether by foot or by transport, public or private.

PITMAN & ASHFIELD    CHARLES TILT    BOOKSELLER    MATTRESS HAIRCUTTER

**46a  Stephenson's Rocket**
Lithograph (93 × 138 mm) by Buxton from the *Mechanic's Magazine* (October, 1829)

**46b  Screening Coals at South Hetton Colliery**
Wood engraving (110 × 145 mm) from the *Penny Magazine* (April, 1835)

'The labouring man, in the present age, if he does but read, has more helps to
wisdom than Solomon had.' The observation comes from the title page of the
*Mechanic's Magazine*; such a journal could be suspected of partiality in its enthusiasm for reading, but the pages which follow are testimony to the truth of the
statement. For his weekly threepence, the *Mechanic's Magazine, Museum, Register,
Journal and Gazette*, to give it its full title, kept the labouring man well informed
of latest developments in various fields of technical advance. It offered 16 pages of
text well illustrated with woodcuts and, for special events, included an extra attrac-
tion. Thus the locomotive competition organised by the directors of the Liverpool
and Manchester Railway was commemorated by a fold-out litho plate depicting
the Rocket and its rivals. For more general instruction, broader in scope if less
topical, the labouring man might subscribe to the *Penny Magazine*, published by
that indefatigable producer of popular literature, Charles Knight, on behalf of the
Society for the Diffusion of Useful Knowledge. A single issue, taken at random,
contains articles on the Carnival at Rome, the loss of the *Royal George*, seal hunting,
the making of Gloucester cheese and wild dogs in Van Diemens Land. The illustration reproduced here is from a series of well-illustrated articles on the industries
of Britain; it has the merit of being not an idealised scene but one sketched on the
spot. Thus even a cheap popular magazine becomes a valuable historical document.

**47a Republican Demonstration at Paris**
Etching (143 × 98 mm) by Hervieu from Frances Trollope's *Paris and the Parisians* (1835)

**47b Jumpers**
Wood engraving (58 × 81 mm) from Nightingale's *Religious Ceremonies of All Nations* (1821)

The Reverend Nightingale, in the preface to his book, gave as his reason for compiling it that existing books on the subject were either inadequate or, in the case of Picart's definitive book (see **17a**), difficult to obtain and prohibitively expensive, costing between £30 and £40 (which in 1835 was worth far more than the £120 that Picart's work was fetching in 1970). In any case much had happened to religion since Picart's time; in particular there had appeared such enthusiastic sects as the Welsh Methodists, known as 'jumpers' for the logical reason that, in pious imitation of David before the Ark of God, they jumped. The newly revived wood engraving was an admirable medium for such an illustration as this, far more expressive than a comparable working of the same subject in metal. Perhaps a similar motive made Hervieu choose etching rather than engraving, but it was probably more a case of artistic snobbery—the French have always had a penchant for this medium. However, he uses the technique so effectively that he cannot be blamed. The freedom of line gives a lighter, livelier result than the more formal engraving; if precision and clarity have been sacrificed, a freshness and spontaneity have been achieved in their place.

**48a  Le Croque-mort**
Steel engraving (80×130 mm) by Louis from a drawing by Monnier for
*Les Français* (1850)

**48b  The Mute**
Wood engraving (108×77 mm) from a drawing by Kenny Meadows for his
*Heads of the People* (1840)

Perhaps it was a symptom of the rise of the bourgeoisie that in the mid-nineteenth
century there was a noticeable tendency to put people in pigeon-holes, assigning
them irrevocably to the stations in life which Providence in its wisdom had ordained
for them. Several artists on both sides of the Channel made collections of character-
types which show, if not what such people looked like, at least what their contemporaries *thought* they should look like. Kenny Meadows' double-faced mute could
have stepped out of the pages of Dickens, Monnier's out of those of Balzac: both
are small-part players in 'la comédie humaine'.

**49a Oxford's Assassination Attempt on Victoria and Albert**
Gypsograph (178×243 mm) from a drawing by Thomas Nicholson (1840)

**49b Waiting for Lloyd's Newspaper**
Wood engraving (118×197 mm) for an advertisement carried in the
part-publications of Dickens' novels (1840s)

Instant news reporting has always been a dream of the publisher: the search for increasingly rapid means of reproduction has been a continuous process, of which the modern culmination is the instantaneity of the television camera. We can only guess at the nature of the gypsographic technique which enabled **49a** to be processed and printed in eight hours. The drawing was presumably made on, or rather into, a block of gypsum, from which a relief plate was taken in some soft metal; this explains the soft outlines and crude shapes. As the plate was only of a soft metal, only a limited number of copies could have been taken before the block was useless; as a news scoop, however, the venture had probably been satisfactory. Two days after the event, which in any case took place in the evening, this picture was on sale to the public. Those who could not afford a copy of their own would, of course, have had to wait their turn to see it at the coffee-house. Our second plate is in fact an unashamed imitation of Haydon's famous picture 'Waiting for the Times, the Morning after the Debate on Reform 8 October 1831'.

The whole subject of the artist as reporter is excellently dealt with in Paul Hogarth's book of that name (Studio Vista, London, 1967).

**50a Soirée at the Duc d'Orleans**
Steel engraving (98 × 165 mm) by Charles Rolls after Eugène Lami, from the collection *A Season in Paris* (about 1840)

**50b Ferdinand Philippe, Duc d'Orleans**
Lithograph (334 × 226 mm) by Basset, probably from his own drawing (about 1840)

Ferdinand, duke of Orleans, was the son of King Louis Philippe and heir to the French throne. He was killed in a riding accident in 1842, so that Basset's portrait almost suggests that he is just setting out on his fatal ride. Though frequently used for portraiture during the nineteenth century, the lithograph was not often employed to better effect than here. The hang of the Duke's coat, and of that of his 'tiger', is, for instance, beautifully rendered by the chalky texture, far more expressively than would have been possible with a line engraving. At the same time we sense no loss in the expressiveness of the features. The placing of the two figures is a *tour de force* which not only is aesthetically satisfying but also makes an eloquent comment on the relationship between man and servant. Lami's picture captures the same elegance in its most characteristic setting—the soirée. It was an age which thought of itself as romantic, and in Lami it found its most sympathetic illustrator. Though celebrated for his paintings of battles and state events, his pictures of daily life are an appropriately romantic reflection of the period as it would have wished to be remembered. He presents a partial, but not inaccurate, view of his age.

L. Bass..

**51a Railway Accident between Tunbridge and Penshurst (1846)** (115 × 160 mm)

**51b A Lady Alpinist (1883)** (300 × 233 mm) after a drawing by R Caton Woodville

**51c Main Drainage Works at Old Ford (1859)** (173 × 240 mm)

Wood engravings from the *Illustrated London News*

It is almost impossible to overestimate the importance of the *Illustrated London News* as a pictorial record. From its founding in 1842 to the present day it has provided a continuous visual commentary on the times. Its ideas of what is significant are open to question, but the total corpus of its work (in its early days each year's issues contained more than 15,000 engravings) adds up to an unparalleled quarry of documentary material. Imitators quickly appeared abroad, in France, Spain, Germany, Russia and America, and rivals in Britain, notably the *Illustrated Times* and the *Graphic*. However, the *Illustrated London News* remains the paradigm by which the others are judged, and it is perhaps significant that it is the only one to have survived to the present day. The pictures we have chosen to exemplify its contribution (three pictures from almost a million) characterise both the high artistic quality of the magazine and the changes of emphasis which gradually affected it during its triumphant career. The first picture is a genuine news event, reported naïvely but vividly, the second is a scene which shows a contemporary happening, but without the urgency of the first, and the third is a picture which could have appeared at any time, without any difference in impact. This selection illustrated the increase in technical accomplishment: the artists and engravers of the *Illustrated London News* soon developed a superlative competence which could at times rise to **a higher artistic** level. The picture of drainage construction is one of the finest scenes of Victorian labourers that can be found (incidentally, it is almost certainly worked up from a photograph.) As for the lady alpinist, she is depicted with the consummate skill expected from one of the magazine's most famous contributors: and if the picture lacks topical significance, it gives us instead a useful and charming glimpse of a small facet of Victorian life.

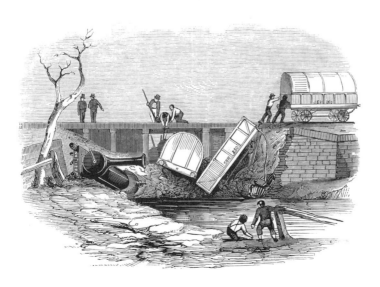

**52a and b** Wood engravings (217 × 330 mm) by George Cruikshank, forming Plates 1 and 4 of his series *The Bottle* (1847)

Cruikshank, the famous illustrator of Dickens, was a lifelong champion of temperance, and produced a continual series of pictorial attacks on the demon drink. None is finer than his celebrated series *The Bottle*, in which he managed for once to curb his instinct for facetious caricature, to produce a set of eight intensely powerful scenes depicting the successive stages of the drunkard's career in highly believable terms. If today one might tend to mock the notion that such disastrous calamities could follow from just 'taking a drop', that is because drunkenness is no longer the social menace it was in Cruikshank's day. For this reformation, Cruikshank's uncompromising propaganda must take some of the credit.

**53a House of Call for the 'Victoria' Audience**
Wood engraving (112 × 152 mm) from G. A. Sala's *Twice Round the London Clock* (1858)

**53b A London Barmaid**
Wood engraving (145 × 120 mm) from a drawing by Gavarni, from his collection *Gavarni in England* (1849)

Throughout the nineteenth century foreign visitors came over to Britain to marvel. They may not always have liked what they saw, but they could not but be fascinated. In general they seldom got beyond London, whose richness and variety attracted them even while its squalor and dirt repelled. Gavarni's observation of the misery and vices of the London poor had a traumatic effect on his work: when he returned to France he was no longer a frivolous social commentator, but concerned himself with deeper and more penetrating investigation of the human condition. Though he makes no direct comment on this scene, the sinister shades of the background suggest his hidden feelings. Similarly the illustrator of Sala's guided tour of London, though he displays a seemingly lively and cheerful public house scene, hints at his personal response in the number of small children he introduces into his picture.

**54a Gasfitters at Work**
Wood engraving (79 × 67 mm) from *The Boy's Book of Trades* (about 1850)

**54b Winding the Cotton Yarn, Nottingham**
Wood engraving (145 × 87 mm) by Paterson from the drawing by Morrow, from
the *English Illustrated Magazine* (1883)

How did ordinary people go about their daily work? Every professional researcher
soon learns that it is easy enough to find pictures of the exceptional, but far harder
to find those of the everyday. *The Boy's Book of Trades* is a rare exception; it sets
out to show how the gasfitter, the decorator, the plumber and other workers went
about their work—what tools they used and how they used them. The chapter on the
gasfitter is typically thorough. It illustrates twenty-six separate tools which he used
in his work, tools which might possibly be in use today, but which have more
probably disappeared, without trace except for such a record as this. The naïve
picture helps us to imagine what it was like when the gasfitter and his mate invaded
a cluttered Victorian home to install the new lighting. As for those workers who
were obliged to work in a factory, the second picture serves as a reminder that child
labour was by no means abolished by Shaftesbury's Factory Act. The accompany-
ing article makes no comment on this scene except to speak patronisingly of the
quiet and modest demeanour of the Nottingham girls compared with that of working women in other English towns.

**55a Building the Crystal Palace**
Wood engraving (165 × 120 mm) from the *Illustrated London News* (1850)

**55b Lady's Work Table in Bogwood** (140 × 90 mm)
**55c Garratt's Thrashing Machine** (96 × 139 mm)
Steel engravings from Great Exhibition commemorative volume (1851)

Prince Albert's plan for a Great Exhibition was received somewhat doubtfully at first, but his enthusiastic promotion of the project eventually roused the British nation to a frenzied combination of pride and curiosity. In journals like the *Illustrated London News* every phase of the construction was followed with eager interest, so that the undertaking is more thoroughly documented than almost any of the great buildings of history. This seemingly artless but actually very carefully drawn view gives us a unique insight into the techniques used. As for the Exhibition itself, it provided an unmatched opportunity to take stock of the achievements of the age, both technological and artistic. For many of the 6,170,000 visitors it was probably their first opportunity to inspect a thrashing machine at close quarters. Less happily, it was also an opportunity for them to absorb some not altogether desirable notions of aesthetic values. However, whatever modern opinion of the respective merits of Garratt's machine and Jones's table may be, these excellent engravings provide a superbly detailed record of a landmark in the growth of national self-awareness.

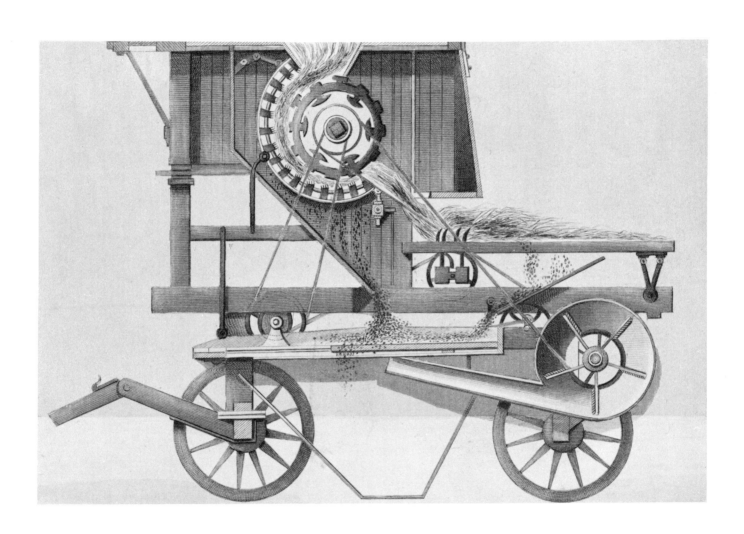

**56a  Dr Baker's Interview with the Yorkshire Factory Girls**
Wood engraving (195 × 250 mm) from a photograph by Baume, in *The British Workman* (1856)

**56b  A Working-Class Home: The Evening Meal**
Wood engraving (193 × 252 mm) from *The British Workman* (1858)

*The British Workman* was a monthly paper selling for one penny, with the avowed aim of discouraging the working classes from drinking, smoking, gambling, striking and lying abed on Sunday. In **56a** the well-meaning Dr Baker has caught a group of factory girls during their lunch break and is exhorting them not to waste their earnings but to deposit them in the savings bank. The object of such saving is shown in the second picture—the ideal working family in its natural habitat. The notice over the mantelpiece proclaims the father to be a member of a temperance society; the books on the shelf, like that which his wife is reading to him, have, no doubt, a high moral content. The blazing fire, the well-provisioned table, are signs that virtue is rewarded not only in the next world but also in this. In the face of such smug piety, one would like to believe that the smile on the left-hand factory girl's face is one of cynical disbelief.

**57a Bancroft's Home at Northampton, Massachusetts**
Steel engraving (90 × 145 mm) by Rolph from a daguerreotype, in *Homes of American Authors* (1857)

**57b The Tombs Prison, New York**
Wood engraving (295 × 225 mm) from a drawing by Arthur Boyd Houghton in the *Graphic* (1870)

The superb quality of American engraving is well exemplified by this attractive Massachusetts landscape, even if for documentary purposes the photograph from which it has been adapted might be preferred. It can be safely assumed that in the photograph Mr Bancroft's house did not stand out quite so clearly from its neighbours, but it is engraver's licence that the sun should shine on the subject of his picture while clouds cast shadow over its surroundings. American readers were not so pleased with the pictures of their country which they saw in the *Graphic*. Founded in 1869 as a rival to the *Illustrated London News*, which it imitates completely in format, the *Graphic* had a policy of maintaining a high standard of graphic work. None of the proprietor's decisions was wiser than to allow Houghton the chance to visit America to make his 'Graphic America' drawings, even though he eventually found that these pictures lost him more subscribers than they won. As reportage, the best of these drawings deserve to rank alongside those of Gustave Doré's *London* for their combination of artistic effect and social impact.

**58a The Engagement between the Merrimac and Monitor, 9 March, 1862**
Steel engraving (118 × 190 mm) by Davies after a drawing by Parsons (1862)

**58b** The same subject: wood engraving (122 × 194 mm) by Evans after a drawing
by Davidson, from the *Century Magazine* (1885)

One of the most momentous battles of history was fought when the Confederate
gunboat *Merrimac*, after causing widespread damage to the Federal Fleet, was
finally challenged by the hastily constructed *Monitor*. For several hours these two
vessels, the first ironclads, kept up the fight, each bombarding the other at close
range with shells incapable of piercing its armour. By nightfall no conclusion had
been reached. Both boats retired battered but unbeaten, but the brief supremacy of
the *Merrimac* was over and a new era of naval warfare had begun. The two illustrations show the great skill of American engravers in both steel and wood. They
illustrate, too, the strong and weak points of each technique. The steel engraving
has an elegance and a precision that the wood cannot attain; the wood achieves a
strength and vitality not to be found in the steel.

**59a  Prostitutes and Clients in the Haymarket, London**
Wood engraving (118 × 165 mm) from Mayhew's *London Labour and the
London Poor* (1850s)

**59b  Female Convicts at Work, Brixton Prison**
Wood engraving (182 × 130 mm) after a photograph by Watkins from Mayhew's
*Criminal Prisons of London* (1862)

Mayhew's *London Labour and the London Poor*, with its sequel, *Criminal Prisons*,
was the outstanding social document of its age—one is tempted to say, of *any* age.
Not only is it crammed full of facts, many of them otherwise unobtainable, about
the social conditions of the working people of London, but it also fills out these
facts with first-hand accounts, gleaned in the course of personal interviews with the
characters described, which anticipate the direct confrontation methods of modern
reporting. The text is copiously illustrated with engravings, many of them based
on photographs, showing various types of street labour, prostitutes and criminals
in their favourite haunts, and the prison life which awaited those who got caught.
These pictures are neither illustrations to moral tracts nor the product of an
emotional outsider's subjective response, but a documentary record which shows us
conditions as they really were. The fact that the book was created at all is the more
surprising since Mayhew was chiefly a humorous writer. One of the founders of
*Punch*, his output chiefly consisted of plays and frivolous fiction, yet it is for his
magnificently human social investigations that he is remembered.

**60a Citizen Raoul Rigault, Prefect of Police during the Paris Commune**
Hand-coloured engraving (165×117 mm) after a drawing by Bertall from his
*Types of the Commune* (1871)

**60b Stonewall Jackson**
Steel engraving (185×143 mm) after a painting by Nast (1862)

Here are two pictures which perform similar functions in utterly different ways
and which typify the special illustrative talents of their respective countries of origin.
Bertall has brilliantly captured the fanatical revolutionary, a medical student turned
communard leader who, before he was himself tried and shot, achieved notoriety
for cold-blooded dedication to his cause. The brisk, blunt lines of the drawing seem
wholly appropriate to their subject. The American general's elegant pose might
seem at odds with his brilliance on the battlefield: but his soldiering and his portrait
have in common a sure-footed professionalism which is the hallmark of Americans
in the arts, including those of engraving and war-making. Bertall's portrait could
hardly have come from any other country but France, and Jackson's portrait could
certainly never have come from anywhere but the United States.

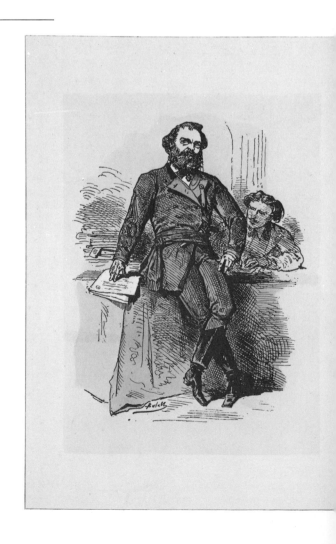

**61a Lowering the Great Winged Bull**
Lithograph (113 × 186 mm) by Walton from Layard's *Nineveh and its Remains* (1848)

**61b Hadrian's Wall at Cockmount Hill**
Lithograph (133 × 189 mm) by Kell from Bruce's *The Roman Wall* (1867)

Was it the association of archaeology with stones which inspired these two illustrators to turn to the lithograph, or were they activated only by aesthetic considerations? Whatever the reason, the choice was a happy one in both cases. Both examples triumph over the lithograph's limited ability to reproduce detail, by giving an excellent expressiveness to their drawing. In addition, they achieve depth by heavier and lighter tones, something which would not have been easy with steel or wood engraving. The sense of perspective in the Roman Wall picture, in particular, is beautifully rendered; compare this with the flat perspective of the otherwise excellent plate of Bancroft's home (**57a**).

**62a Faraday Lecturing**
Wood engraving (137 × 202 mm) from a Sunday magazine (about 1846)

**62b Experiment with Electricity**
Wood engraving (76 × 85 mm) from a popular scientific textbook translated
from the French (about 1870)

**62c Andrew Ure Galvanising a Murderer's Corpse, 4 November, 1818**
Wood engraving (105 × 140 mm) from Louis Figuier's *Merveilles de la science* (1867)

The British talked a lot about science, as our picture of Faraday illustrates, but it
was the French above all who wrote about it. In the field of 'la vulgarisation de la
science' they were pre-eminent, particularly as a result of the work of Louis Figuier,
from whose superb *Merveilles de la science* the picture of Ure is taken. It is not a
very good picture—French wood engravers were seldom great artists—but it is
probably the only existing illustration of this subject. The same rarity value applies
to many of the subjects that Figuier and his compatriots dealt with—from primitive
man and the Flood to the latest developments in electric traction, not omitting
spiritualism and the manufacture of Roquefort cheese. Most English textbooks of
the period were translated from the French and used their pictures; this accounts for
the very un-English dress of the two lads demonstrating how, by standing on an
insulating stool, one person can transmit an electric current to his neighbour.

As background to **62c** it may be added that Andrew Ure carried out his experiments in
galvanism at Glasgow University. He arranged the purchase of the corpse of the murderer
Clydesdale with the man himself, the day before his execution. The body hung for nearly
an hour before being cut down: ten minutes later it had been rushed to the anatomy
laboratory at the University and connected to a Voltaic pile. The effects of connecting
the current to various parts of the body were so horrifying that many of those present had
to leave the room. But Ure did not succeed, as he had hoped, in bringing the man back to
life again.

a

b

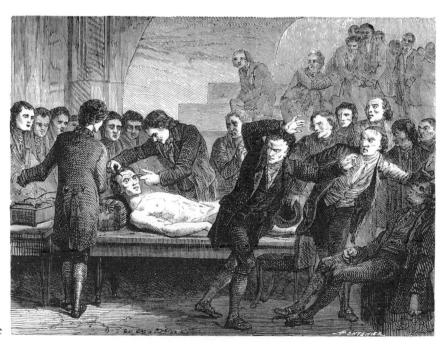

c

**63a  Rotten Row, Hyde Park** (58 × 167 mm)

**63b  Kensington Gardens** (235 × 188 mm) by Pannemaker

**63c  Coffee Stall, Early Morning** (241 × 195 mm) by H. Pisan

Wood engravings from drawings by Gustave Doré for his *London* (1871)

Gustave Doré was one of the most prolific artists of all time. He was widely published before he was 20, found fame at 22 with his edition of Rabelais, and continued to pour out a stream of paintings and illustrations for more than thirty years. He has left a series of splendidly illustrated books, including a magnificent Dante and a no less magnificent Bible, but none displays his genius better than his most documentary work, *London*, created after touring the sunshine and shadows of that city with Blanchard Jerrold in 1869. He drew with great facility directly on to the wood block, which he then passed over to an engraver. Some of his collaborators, such as Pisan and Pannemaker (the work of both is represented here), must have been considerable artists in their own right, for the brilliance of the original vision is translated into the language of engraving with almost uncanny skill. The result is a matchless document: a city at the height of the Industrial Revolution, seething in its own social revolution, portrayed with an artistry which amplifies each picture's message rather than, as so often happens, muting it.

a

b

c

**64a  Miss Laura Clarendon and Friends**
Wood engraving (170 × 240 mm) from *The Day's Doings* (1871)

**64b  A Drama of Vitriol**
Wood engraving (303 × 267 mm), signed Beltrand, from *Le Petit Parisien* (1897)

*The Day's Doings* is almost identical in appearance to the *Illustrated London News*, but its conception of what constitutes news is very different. Take, for instance, the item about Miss Laura Clarendon, a lady of some reputation in certain Glasgow circles. She happened to be entertaining a few friends when, in response to complaints from her neighbours, the police burst in, to find her giving one of her celebrated performances as a pretty horse-breaker, whip and all. The number of empty bottles shows what stage the party had reached, though beyond a certain disarrangement of the neckwear none of the company had as yet dispensed with his or her clothing. This is good spicy stuff, but one has only to compare it with the second illustration to see how much more seriously the French took their scandal. The readers of *Le Petit Parisien* were treated to two such pictures every week; if they also subscribed to its indistinguishable rival *Le Petit Journal*, they received four. With the same graphic realism sensational events of all kinds were reported—the assassination of presidents, fires in menageries, electrocutions, Channel flights, all were drawn and engraved to standards of workmanship higher than those applied by the French to any other field of illustration.

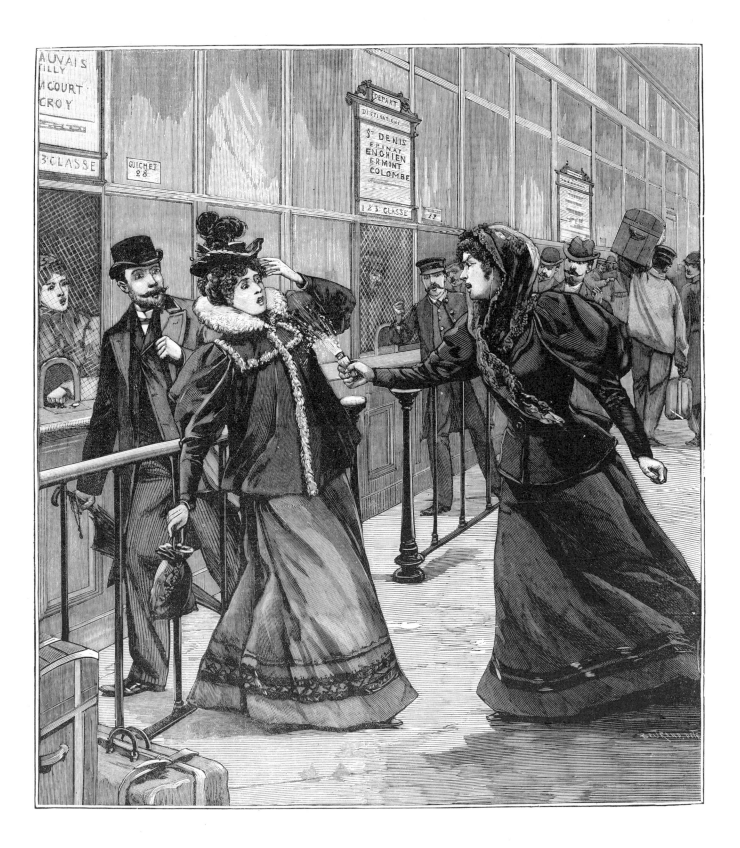

143

**65a Undergraduates Making a Road as Suggested by Mr Ruskin** (305 × 450 mm) (1874)

**65b The Out-patients' Room, University College Hospital** (305 × 450 mm) (1872)

Wood engravings from the *Graphic*

The great events of history come and go, scandals erupt and are soon forgotten, but everyday life is always in progress. It has been shown (**51**) how the emphasis of the *Illustrated London News* shifted from hard news to soft reportage over the years. One of the forces stimulating this shift must have been the success of the *Graphic*, which from its start in 1869 took a special interest in mirroring the life of its readers. Its pages are full of splendid drawings like these, many of which deserve to rank beside the better-known paintings of the Victorian domestic genre.

**66  The Duchess of Edinburgh Arrives at Windsor, 1874**
As seen by (**a**) the *Illustrated London News* (212×312 mm) and (**b**) the *Graphic* (225×300 mm)

**67a** Cartoon (200 × 160 mm) by John Tenniel in *Punch* (1885)

**67b** Cartoon (378 × 242 mm) by Hal Ludlow in *Judy* (1889)

Political caricature in Victorian days seems emasculated when compared with the genre in the great days of Rowlandson and Gillray. Yet what it lacked in vigour it often gained in wit. Tenniel, though chiefly remembered as the illustrator of *Alice*, was best known to his contemporaries as a political cartoonist, the mainstay of this art in *Punch* for many decades. His drawing of the perpetually optimistic Gladstone is delightfully economical, and very reminiscent of his *Alice* illustrations. Ludlow's drawing for *Judy*, though, is a more satisfying piece of work, a stunning drawing which achieves tremendous impact despite its simple, restrained treatment. *Judy*, a late rival to *Punch*, ran for several years. While it never equalled its competitor in the possession of such fine artists as Leech, Keene and du Maurier, it compensated for this by the excellence of its political drawings, which are generally more highly finished and carefully worked out than those in *Punch*, and deserve to be much better known.

**68a Roast Pheasant with Truffles**
Steel engraving (92 × 144 mm) from Gustave Garlin's *Le Cuisinier moderne* (1887)

**68b Salter's Household Specialities**
Advertisement page (262 × 164 mm) from the *Ironmonger Diary and Text Book* (1889)

Where are the kitchen gadgets of former days? Solidly made of cast iron, they would seem to have been indestructible; yet one would probably comb the antique shops of Britain in vain for Hughes's patent Fountain Clothes Washer. Thus advertisements such as this are often the only record of the aids to gracious living available to the Victorian housewife. Every one of these illustrations—and the *Ironmonger Diary* alone contains many hundreds—had to be drawn by an artist, then engraved. Knowing that he would use the cuts many times, the advertiser would probably then make metal blocks of them, to be inserted in advertisements and catalogues as required. Even more ephemeral than these kitchen utensils were the dishes those kitchens produced. What modern housewife, anxious to offer her husband something different for supper, turns to Garlin's gastronomic tome for inspiration? This *tour de force* has been chosen almost at random from his pages: it is in fact one of the *less* spectacular of the creations that he describes.

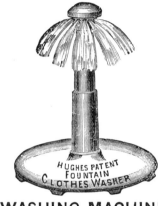

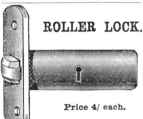

**69a Emigrants**

Wood engraving (137 × 204 mm) by Derbier after the painting by Dawant (1887)

**69b A Fight in the Street**

Process engraving (95 × 125 mm) from a drawing by Frederic Remington, illustrating Theodore Roosevelt's 'Frontier Types' (*Century Magazine*, October, 1888)

This pair of pictures reveals a paradox that gives another salutary lesson in the pitfalls of illustration. On one hand, a picture (**69a**) whose photographic naturalism almost conveys the impression of complete factual authenticity, except that the artist has tried too hard for this illusion, and the spectator's credibility rebels. On the other, Remington's presentation of that obligatory scene from every Western film, the fight outside the saloon, seems at first sight to be as far from reality as those films, until it is remembered that this is the factual source from which Hollywood drew its inspiration, that this in fact *is* the Wild West.

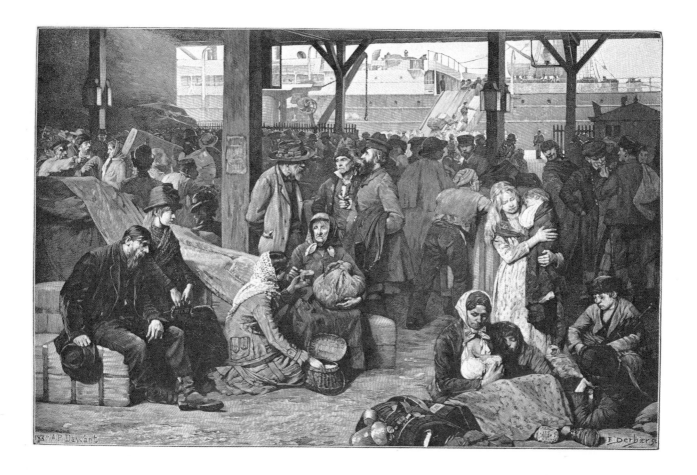

**70a Bridge over the English Channel**
Engraving (150×220 mm) from *La Science illustrée* (1889)

**70b Spaceship in Trouble over the Moon**
Engraving (172×170 mm) by Fernand Fau from Le Faure's *Les Robinsons lunaires* (1893)

The French imagination triumphs again! Schneider and Hersent's Channel Bridge project, seemingly the more easily realisable of these two dreams, remains a dream after a further eighty years. But the modern age can check the accuracy of Le Faure's fantastic drama. It has seen what for him was the future, and if Le Faure's conjectures have proved inaccurate, let us at least praise him and his imaginative fellow-countrymen for helping our imagination to escape from the world of things as they are into the world of things as they might be.

Illustrations of the kinds shown in this book can be obtained from a variety of sources—some of them predictable, some less obvious. Professional picture researchers keep notebooks crammed with useful addresses, ranging from public collections large and small to private individuals who possess hoards of pictures on specific subjects, often containing material no museum can match. Between these two categories is a third, the commercial picture libraries, some general, others specialist: these as a rule house their material in a convenient and accessible form, and are generally geared to meeting the needs of the professional or amateur researcher; but of course they do not often possess the treasures gathered in the museums.

To compile a comprehensive file of these sources would be virtually impossible—certainly no researcher's notebook would be fat enough to hold them. In any case, for the average picture-hunter, such a list would be confusing and bewildering. So what we have set out to do here is indicate the most useful primary sources, which should meet most needs and provide a starting point for any search. Which of these sources should you try first? Geography apart, your choice could be influenced by various factors. If you are in a hurry, you will sometimes find the public collections frustratingly slow. On the other hand, if cost is a critical factor, they are generally (though not always) cheaper than the commercial libraries. If you are good at charming custodians into granting you the use of their facilities, you may find some of the more recondite sources are not quite so formidable as they at first appear. If you need help in making your selection, commercial libraries are more likely to put themselves out for you, if only because they have a financial interest in so doing.

## BUYING YOUR OWN PICTURES

Surprisingly enough, this can often be the cheapest way as well as the most satisfying: unfortunately it is also the least certain. You may be lucky, and find the picture you are looking for at very little cost, but the chances of finding it at the moment when you need it are very much against you. The seventeenth-century woodcut shown in plate **6a** was bought on a Paris quai for about five francs, but that was a piece of luck. After being undervalued for nearly half a century, prices of prints are rising rapidly at present, but in London, New York, Paris and Amsterdam, for example, there are print shops where you can still buy illustrative material of the highest quality at modest prices; generally speaking, the more knowledgeable the dealer, the fairer his prices are likely to be. All the same, bargains are still to be found in bookshops and antique shops, so it pays to nose about in their dusty corners.

## PUBLIC COLLECTIONS

Most major collections of books and pictures will allow illustrative material to be copied and reproduced, under certain conditions and at a fee which is usually modest. The cheapest way to borrow an illustration is to hunt it out for yourself in such public collections as the British Museum in London, the Bibliothèque Nationale in Paris or the Library of Congress in Washington. Each museum has its own regulations, and familiarity with their procedure can save much time and frustration. If you know precisely which picture you want, or from what book it is taken, and if possible its catalogue number, the process of securing it need not take very long. You can either write for a print or make a personal call (in the latter case you often require a reader's ticket, generally provided free of charge). If the picture has already been photographed, you may get a copy on the spot or within a short space of time, otherwise you may have to wait weeks or even months. In some museums it will be up to you to arrange for a photographer to make the copy; sometimes this service is provided by the museum. Usually there is a reproduction fee to be paid when the picture is used: in some cases this fee will vary according to the purpose for which it is used, and may be waived in exceptional circumstances. If you are looking generally for pictures to illustrate a subject, and have no specific illustrations in mind, a personal search is essential. Supplying such material is only a secondary function of the collection, and the staff cannot spare the time to give you more than limited assistance. The better organised collections have subject indexes, which are of course extremely helpful, but even for a professional, searching for pictures in public collections is apt to be a laborious and frustrating experience.

## Great Britain

### BRITISH MUSEUM PRINT ROOM
Great Russell Street, London WC1. Telephone 01-636 1555.
General subjects from the fifteenth century onwards, prints and drawings by specific artists. Comprehensively indexed. The print collection is backed by one of the world's largest collections of books and periodicals from all countries and periods, from which material can be photocopied on request. Photographers visit regularly and will take photographs on request: the librarians will give advice about them. For personal visits, a ticket is required (obtaining this will take at least 24 hours.) Reproduction fees are chargeable over and above print fees. The librarians will answer simple inquiries on the phone.

### BODLEIAN LIBRARY, WESTERN MANUSCRIPTS DEPARTMENT
Oxford. Telephone 0865 44675.
All aspects of life between 800 and 1520. Subject indexes. Reader's ticket or acceptable letter of introduction required. Photographic facilities available. Print fee charged but no reproduction fee.

### NATIONAL PORTRAIT GALLERY
2 St Martin's Place, London WC2. Telephone 01-930 8511.
Portraits of notable people throughout British history. Printed catalogue of portraits for sale at main desk. Negatives held of portraits from other galleries or in private ownership, from which prints can be obtained when permission has been granted.

### GUILDHALL LIBRARY
Guildhall, London EC2. Telephone 01-606 3030.
A large well-indexed collection covering a wide range of subjects. Items lent, or they can be photographed. No appointment or ticket required. No reproduction fee.

### VICTORIA AND ALBERT MUSEUM
South Kensington, London SW7. Telephone 01-589 6371.
Large collection on a wide range of subjects. Print room staff very helpful on simple telephone inquiries. No tickets or appointments necessary for print room, but

reader's ticket required for library which contains many illustrated books. Photographic services available, or you can arrange for your own.

Other London museums, such as the SCIENCE MUSEUM, the NATIONAL MARITIME MUSEUM and the IMPERIAL WAR MUSEUM, contain material on specific subjects which is available on certain conditions.

Regional libraries and museums contain material relating to the appropriate area, including topography and history, in particular:

WALES National Library of Wales, Aberystwyth, Cardiganshire
SCOTLAND Scottish National Portrait Gallery, Queen St, Edinburgh 2
NORTHERN IRELAND Ulster Museum, Stranmillis, Belfast
ISLE OF MAN Manx Museum and Art Gallery, Douglas, I.O.M.

Learned societies generally have their own libraries, and sometimes picture collections, which are usually accessible to the public for purposes of illustration. The ROYAL GEOGRAPHICAL SOCIETY, the SOCIETY FOR PSYCHICAL RESEARCH and the like should be approached directly for help in specific fields.

Local libraries frequently house specialist collections which are available to the public, usually at a nominal fee. A guide to these is available at most public libraries.

**United States**

LIBRARY OF CONGRESS, PRINTS AND PHOTOGRAPHS DIVISION
Washington 25, D.C.
General subjects from fifteenth century to present, emphasis on American history. No reproduction fees. Catalogue available.

PIERPONT MORGAN LIBRARY
29-33 East 36th Street, New York 16, N.Y.
All varieties of illustrative material covering medieval and renaissance periods to the nineteenth century. Print fees charged: reproduction or copyright fees are the client's responsibility.

MUSEUM OF THE CITY OF NEW YORK, PRINT DEPARTMENT
Fifth Avenue and 103rd Street, New York 29, N.Y.
Varied material from 1626 to present day, emphasis on history of New York City and its environs.

NEW YORK PUBLIC LIBRARY
Fifth Avenue and 42nd Street, New York 18, N.Y.
Wide collection under subject headings. No reproduction fee.

FREE LIBRARY OF PHILADELPHIA, RARE BOOK DEPARTMENT
AND PRINT AND PICTURE DEPARTMENT
Logan Square, Philadelphia 3, Pa.
Wide variety of material, particular emphasis on American history, portraits, geography.

Public libraries in the United States are not only excellent sources of original material relating to their region, but often contain special collections of particular subjects, e.g., the Denver Public Library houses the Ross-Barrett collection on the history of aeronautics. Most of these can be found in the book *Picture Sources* listed at the end of this chapter.

**France**

BIBLIOTHÈQUE NATIONALE, Cabinet des Estampes
58 rue Richelieu, Paris 2 Telephone 542 00-06
Wide variety of material on all subjects from 1400 to the present. Reproduction fees charged.

CAISSE NATIONALE DES MONUMENTS HISTORIQUES
Grand Palais, Porte F, Cours la Reine, Paris 8. Telephone 359 45-95.
Works of art from the museums of France. Reproduction fees charged.

**Germany**

For historical reasons, German material tends to be widely scattered in regional centres. Individual town-halls and local museums frequently contain the best material. Among the more generally useful are these:

RHEINISCHES BILDARCHIV
Museum of the City of Cologne
Zeughausstrasse 1-3, (5) Köln, West Germany.
Artistic and cultural history of the Rhineland.

STAATSBIBLIOTHEK
Der Stiftung Preussicher Kulturbesitz-Bildarchiv
1 Berlin, Postfach 59, West Germany.

BUNDESARCHIV KOBLENZ
Am Wollershof 12, Postfach 320, West Germany.

**Italy**

KUNSTHISTORISCHES INSTITUT IN FLORENZ
Piazza S. Spirito 9, Firenze.
Italian fine arts and architecture from antiquity to the present day.

MUSEO CIVICO DI VENEZIA, Archivo Fotografico
Piazza San Marco 52, Venezia.
Venetian art and history 1200-1800.

## PUBLISHERS, PHOTOGRAPHERS, AGENCIES

If the picture you want has already been used in another book, you may be able to short-cut the normal process of seeking the original source by going either to the publisher of the book or to the photographer or agency who copied the original. Some publishers have their own libraries, containing pictures which they have used in their books, and which they are in some cases willing to lend out at a specified fee. Alternatively, you can follow up the credit supplied in the book and contact the photographer who copied the pictures and who may hold the print. (Commercial agencies in Britain are listed in *Writers and Artists Year Book*, published annually by A & C Black). You will still of course have to clear the rights to use the picture, but at least you will have the picture itself.

## COMMERCIAL PICTURE LIBRARIES

Professional as well as non-professional researchers frequently find the commercial picture libraries the most convenient source of illustration, because their facilities save time and thus outweigh the fact that their fees are generally (though not always) higher than those of the public collections. This is because the fee includes the cost of searching. Note that many commercial libraries will reduce their rates when large quantities are used.

A typical commercial collection will have its pictures conveniently filed by subject. Most will send you a selection on request; all will carry out a reasonable amount of research for you within their collections, and some will allow you to browse there for yourself. Often you will be able to borrow a selection of pictures for a reasonable period, paying a reproduction fee only for those you eventually use. Some collections—notably the Mansell and Mary Evans collections in London—lend originals: others supply photocopies, and if a picture has not previously been photocopied you may have to wait a few days for your prints. Some collections charge a small search fee, or a holding fee if pictures are retained beyond a certain time-limit.

These collections offer a service geared to professional needs, since the lending out of pictures is—unlike that of museums—their primary function. Where time is important, they are the preferred source. In some cases you can obtain an illustration in a matter of hours without even making a personal call. Most collections will send you details of facilities and rates on request; they are generally ready to take a personal interest in your needs and to give you advice.

### Great Britain

MANSELL COLLECTION
42 Linden Gardens, London W2. Telephone 01-229 5475.
All subjects, all periods to 1940s. Originals or photocopies supplied. Write, phone or personal visit (by appointment). Browsers welcome.

MARY EVANS PICTURE LIBRARY
11 Granville Park, London SE13. Telephone 01-852 5040.
All subjects, all periods to 1900. Originals supplied in most cases. Write, phone or personal visit (preferably by appointment). Research service available for material not held in collection. Browsers welcome.

RADIO TIMES HULTON LIBRARY
35 Marylebone High Street, London W1M 4AA. Telephone 01-580 5577.

All subjects, all periods to about 1950. Photocopies supplied. Write, phone or personal visit (by appointment).

WEAVER SMITH COLLECTION
Thames Television, 306 Euston Road, London NW1. Telephone 01-387 9494.
Varied subjects seventeenth, eighteenth and nineteenth centuries. Write, phone or personal visit.

*Specialist collections:*
RAYMOND MANDER AND JOE MITCHENSON THEATRE COLLECTION
5 Venner Road, London SE26. Telephone 01-778 6730.
All aspects of theatre and entertainment.
Write, phone or personal visit (by appointment).

RONAN PICTURE LIBRARY
Ballards Place, Cowlings, Newmarket, Suffolk. Telephone 0440-82 328.
History of science and technology. Write or phone in first instance.

## United States

BETTMAN ARCHIVE
136 East 57th Street, New York 22, N.Y.
All subjects, all periods to 1920. Catalogue available.

BROWN BROTHERS
220 West 42nd Street, New York 36, N.Y.
All subjects, all periods.

CULVER PICTURES
660 First Avenue, New York 16, N.Y.
All subjects, all periods. Subject list available.

HISTORICAL PICTURES SERVICE
2753 West North Avenue, Chicago 47, Illinois.
All historical subjects to 1930.

MERCURY ARCHIVES
1574 Crossroads of the World, Hollywood 28, California.
All subjects, all periods.

## France

ESTABLISHMENT BULLOZ
21 rue Bonaparte, Paris 6. Telephone 326 54-76.
General subjects of all period, emphasis on art. Catalogue available.

GIRAUDON PHOTOGRAPHIE
9 rue des Beaux Arts, Paris 6. Telephone 326 93-83.
Art, history, archaeology. Catalogue available.

ROGER VIOLLET
6 rue de Seine, Paris 6. Telephone 033 81-10.
All subjects, all periods.

SNARK INTERNATIONAL
47 rue Vivienne, Paris 2.
General subjects, emphasis on art.

**Germany**

BILDERDIENST IM SÜDDEUTSCHEN VERLAG
Sendlinger Strasse 80, München 3, West Germany. Telephone 240151.
All subjects, all periods.

MARBURG BILDARCHIV FOTO
Ernst von Hülsen-Haus, Marburg/Lahn, West Germany. Telephone 2770.
Art and architecture of all periods, including engravings.

ULLSTEIN BILDERDIENST
1000 Berlin. Postfach 11.
General subjects.

**Italy**

SCALA
via Chiantigianna, Ponte Arniccheri, 50011 Antella, Firenze. Telephone 641 543.
Chiefly artistic subjects, from museums and galleries throughout Europe.

**USSR (agency in Britain)**
NOVOSTI PRESS AGENCY
3 Rosary Gardens, London SW7. Telephone 01-373 7350.
Hold some material, act as agents for other, on all subjects relating to Russia.

## FREELANCE RESEARCHERS

If your needs are highly specialised, or the search likely to be laborious, it is often economical to employ a professional researcher. There are many freelance researchers available: most publishers have a number of names on their files, and any of the commercial collections will make recommendations. Some commercial collections offer research facilities of their own for material which they do not themselves possess. Employing professional researchers is apt to seem more expensive at first sight, but their first-hand expertise and knowledge of sources can save so much time that this is often the most economical method. Fees are based on the number of pictures found or—more fairly—on hours worked.

**Some useful books**

If there were one book which provided a comprehensive guide to the world's sources of illustration, this chapter would not have been necessary. In the absence of any such, the following works, dealing with limited areas, may be of some value.

*Picture Sources* Ed. Celestine Frankenburg. Special Libraries Association, New York. (Latest edition, 1964). Should be available for consultation at most major libraries. Comprehensive as regards United States, very sketchy elsewhere.

*World of Learning* Europa Publications, London (annually since 1947). Lists museums, learned societies, universities, galleries, etc.

*Picture Source Book for Social History* Allen & Unwin, London, 1961. A 6-volume epic with a wealth of pictures, indicating their sources.

*Guide to the Special collections of prints and photographs in the Library of Congress.* Paul Vanderbilt. Government Printing Office, Washington.

*Museums and Galleries in Great Britain and Ireland.* Published annually by Index, Dunstable, Bedfordshire. Generally available in bookshops.

*International Directory of Arts* (10th edition 1970) Deutsche Zentraldruckerei A.G., Berlin, West Germany. An exhaustive 2-volume directory of museums, galleries, universities, academies, collections, associations, dealers, publishers, collectors, etc., throughout the world.